English for Consultants

Expressions, Phrases, and Cases to Be an Effective Team Player

ADAMA KOMOU

Copyright © 2020 by Adama Komou

All rights reserved.

No part of this book can be reproduced in any form or by any electronic or mechanical means, including information storage and retrieval systems, without permission in writing from the publisher, except by a reviewer who may cite brief passages in a review.

ENGLISH FOR CONSULTANTS: Expressions, Phrases, and Cases to Be an Effective Team Player

Design by Licorne Management Sarl
Images by ZdenekSasek on VectorStock.com

To my parents,

Nathalie and Lassina Komou.

List of Cases

CASE 1: Internal Meeting Transcript — 42

CASE 2: IT Analyst Position Interview — 123

CASE 3: General Practitioner Position Interview — 125

CASE 4: Marketing Manager Position Interview — 125

CASE 5: Finance Analyst Position Interview — 127

CASE 6: AirBed&Breakfast (AirBnB) Pitch Deck — 141

CASE 7: UberCab's Pitch Deck — 145

CASE 8: BIONADE's Market Entry in China (Fictive) — 218

List of Boxes

Box 1: 5 Rules to Be an Effective Team Player	23
Box 2: The Psychology of Pitching	140
Box 3: 7 Golden Rules for Pitching	145
Box 4: 4 Styles of Policy Advocacy Practice	156
Box 5: 4 Rationales of Social Policy Advocacy	158
Box 6: 6-Step Advocacy Engagement Process	160
Box 7: Top 5 Reasons Why Startups Fail	180

Table of Contents

List of Cases iv

List of Boxes v

Preface ix

CHAPTER 1: MEET 1

    Prepare 2

    Request 5

    Open 17

    Agree 24

    Disagree 27

    Interrupt 29

    Ask Opinion 31

    Clarify 33

    Make a Point 35

    Give a Reason 37

    Report Progress 38

    Report Regress 39

    Moderate 40

    Close 40

    Exercises 45

CONTENTS

CHAPTER 2: TALK 46
   Greet Differently 47
   Express Gratitude Differently 51
   Diversify Your English 55
   Make Great Conversations 64
   Expressions for Small Talks 72
   Speak Like an Executive 81
   Talk to Your Team 86
   Speak Like a Consultant 91
   Learn More Transition Words 107
   Exercises 120

CHAPTER 3: IMPRESS 122
   Interview for Jobs 123
   Propose Value 129
   Sell Your Products 134
   Pitch Your Project 140
   Advocate for Reforms 155
   Exercises 161

CHAPTER 4: NEGOTIATE 162
   On Agreement, Deal, or offer 164
   On Your Negotiating Team 167
   On the Counterpart 169
   On Reactions 170
   On Actions 172

CONTENTS

    Exercises 175
CHAPTER 5: DESCRIBE 176
    Describe Your Performance and Scorecard 177
    Words for Recruiters 182
    Words for Work 186
    Define Problems 196
    Exercises 206
CHAPTER 6: ANALYZE 207
    Trends 208
    Analytical Engagements and Problem-Solving 215
    Acronyms, Models, and Indicators 223
    Exercises 232
About the Author 234
Bibliography 237

Preface

I don't have a bachelor's degree in the English language.

A couple of years ago, I was struggling to find a short and comprehensive book that would allow me to add value quickly as a non-native aspiring management consultant. I wondered why English books looked so *academic*, and if some people were feeling the same.

I had to go through many books and courses with no time available. Down the line, I came to reach a plateau. I couldn't seem to make any improvement out of my additional readings and speaking. I started putting together my English toolbox of words, expressions, ideas, and phrases to break the plateau and reach the executive English-speaking level.

Meanwhile, I discovered that high-level business professionals don't *speak* English; they *compile a code of thinking*. Ever since, the whole paradigm in which I was learning shifted. I found that if you wanted to *speak* like an executive, you would first need to *crack their code of thinking*. This finding confirmed when I got into top professional environments, first in consulting, and then at the World Bank.

I thought I should share my experience to provide a *less academic* peer-to-peer way of learning executives' business English, with a shorter learning curve as well.

In this book, I am trying to give you a unique immersion in that code of thinking, using a simple layout that allows the quickest learning. In every chapter, you will uncover a part of the code and resolutely become an *effective team player*.

PREFACE

You have six chapters in the book:

- MEET
- TALK
- IMPRESS
- NEGOTIATE
- DESCRIBE
- ANALYZE

Being an effective communicator in English is a sign of intelligence and productivity. It is highly valuable in competitive environments where you come across a lot of brilliant people. You want to find the best words to communicate all the creativity, intelligence, humor, and wisdom you have got. Eventually, you would change people's minds, win jobs, win negotiations, or business contracts.

This book allows you to dive into an organized immersion with very realistic samples. Whether you are operating in startups, business development, project management, or human resource management, it will help you work more effectively. If you succeed, you will love working in English more than ever.

I think it's worth mentioning that this book doesn't mean to teach you the consulting trade per se. I assume you are already well versed in your field of competence, so I will not dwell on theory or concepts.

Finally, this is not an exhaustive book, as you will not find everything in it. However, it is a good benchmark for non-native (and native) professionals.

PREFACE

Who Is This Book For?

This book is for pre-intermediate non-native (and native) professionals who are struggling to fully deploying their talent and value in a competitive English-speaking professional environment.

This includes, but is not limited to:

- Managers
- Consultants
- Business Analysts
- HR professionals
- Marketers
- Accountants
- Engineers
- Economists
- Non-profit professionals
- Trainers
- Militaries
- Career changers
- Students

Common Works You Will Improve

After reading this book, you will dramatically improve your speaking for:

- Presentations

PREFACE

- Meetings
- Job interviews
- Negotiation rounds
- Technical discussions
- Conversations
- And more

You will also produce better professional texts and communications. For instance, you will improve on:

- Business reports
- Proposals
- Articles
- Essays
- Personal memos
- Notes and emails

How to Benefit from This Book

When it comes to learning, we all have our learning styles. Some of us are visual learners, others are kinesthetic, and several people are auditive learners. In addition to your approach to learning, I suggest to:

- Make at least one cover to cover skimming
- Read the relevant chapter before any related task, to recall all the ideas, words, and expressions
- Read out loud or read with your lips trying to speak out
- Always imagine a situation where you apply expressions
- Memorize a few phrases for deliberate practice
- Re-read the chapters several times
- Complete exercises

Icons Used in This Book

PREFACE

✓ Listing
💬 Spoken expression
📄 Written expression
⏱ Quantitative point
🔄 Qualitative point
♞ A common practice of consultants
📒 Example

Fictive Names Used in This Book

ABC will stand for *"Always Be Consulting."*

Fictive company and project names include:

- ABC Consulting/Client
- ABC Project/Client
- Fintech Project/Client
- Valorization Project/Client
- Water Project/Client
- Food Project/Client
- Health Project/Client
- Turnaround Project/Client
- Private Equity Project/Client
- Investment Fund Project/Client
- Pharmaceutical Project/Client
- New Drug Project
- Fly The World

***Important Notice

No information shared in this book is from my former/current employer nor any previous/existing client.

This page is intentionally left blank.

Chapter 1
MEET

English is not a science. It's a skill. Don't study it. Use it.
Mikhail Kotykhov

MEET

Prepare

⇒ It's a Meeting Or:

gathering	appointment	rendezvous	reunion
assembly	session	event	consultation
encounter	date	talk	rally
convention	summit	interview	discussion

⇒ Different Types of Meeting

annual general meeting	progress meeting	decision meeting	review meeting
negotiation meeting	informational meeting	kickoff meeting	shareholder meeting
board meeting	team meeting	monthly meeting	weekly meeting
breakfast meeting	luncheon meeting	dinner meeting	workshop

MEET

brainstorming	one on one	video conferencing	group discussion
focus group	job fair	the grapevine	business luncheon
networking luncheon	work luncheon	awards luncheon	media luncheon
press luncheon	conference	symposium	seminar

⇒ Reasons for Meetings

review progress collectively	approve a proposition or project	react to changes or events	share or discuss new information
communicate efficiently	amend a document	develop options	approve plans and reports
exercise a legal responsibility	make decisions	solve problems	find and confront ideas
launch a project	raise awareness on some matters	prepare documents	validate a report

⇒ Checklist for Informal Meetings

- Date and time
- Meeting room or place
- Length
- Agenda outline

⇒ Checklist for Formal Meeting

- Terms of reference
- Meeting room and site booking
- Meeting creation in the system
- Invitation letters or emails
- Detailed agenda shared with participants
- Accounting and finance matters
- Trips and hotel management
- Procurement and vendor management
- Stationery and other furniture
- Video projector and projection screen
- Logistics and in-city transportation facilities
- Identity, rank, and origin of guests
- Welcoming of distinguished guests
- Speeches, attendance sheet, and minutes
- Coffee and lunch break services
- Dinner and cocktail services

Request

In Speaking

- Let's schedule a meeting for Monday to cover the details.
- Why not having a meeting tomorrow to discuss the options?
- Could we meet to go through the problem that just cropped up?
- Should we schedule a time to meet with the VC (venture capitalist)?
- Let's schedule a meeting sometime next week to discuss what can be done.
- The best thing to do is to have a meeting with Jack to set the record straight.
- Could we organize a team meeting for next Monday at the building site at 3 PM?
- Perhaps we could meet and go around all the implications of this new piece of legislation.

MEET

💬 I am Alan Ross from ABC Consulting, and I would like to have a meeting with you to discuss something of interest for both of us.

In Writing

📄 Hi,

Hope you are very well. I am from Bangalore and I live in Brooklyn for three years now. Please let me know if you get time to share coffee. (1)

Thank you,
Arun

📄 Hi,

Hope all is well with you. I also graduated from the London School of Economics, and I am currently working in Paris. Please let me know if you have time to share a cup of wine. (1)

Thanks a lot,
Brian

📄 Dear Colleagues,

The next monthly meeting will take place on May 15, 2019, at ABC Consulting Headquarters in Paris. The theme of the meeting will be "Knowledge Management."

I encourage you to send your Practice Improvement Note by May 05, 2019.

All the best,
Cheng

MEET

📎 Dear Robert,

I am writing to invite you to the 2nd Annual Global Operational Improvement Summit, set to take place in San Francisco on June 10th - 12th, 2018. Please find attached the event's agenda.

Here is an outline:

- Organizational improvement Scorecard
- Case study presentations
- Panel discussions
- Breakout sessions

Day two will focus exclusively on interactive workshops hosted by the Fairmont San Francisco Hotel.

ABC will also be launching its first Excellence Award Night to showcase and honor the most outstanding organizational and individual achievements through the application of the Baldrige Organizational Excellence Framework.

Yours truly,
Harry

📎 Dear colleagues,

We would like to invite you to join the upcoming staff briefings hosted by HR regarding the recent International Footprint updates communicated by senior management. The presentations are open to all staff.

During the session, we will share details on several HR policy measures that are part of an overall effort to support the firm's international development.

The proposals mainly cover two areas – (a) how to strengthen global mobility benefits and (b) how to better facilitate global careers for staff.

This event is an early opportunity for HR to have your takes.

We look forward to your participation.

Best regards,
Alicia

Dear colleagues,

We would like to invite you to the Decision Meeting for the ABC project. The meeting will be held on Monday, November 25, from 11:30 am to 1:00 pm UTC, in room 15 at Hong Kong with connections to Boston, New Delhi, and Johannesburg. Please see the connection details below.

Andrew Carlson (Partner, Boston), Arjun Singh (Partner, New York), and Christine Dupont (Director, Paris) will chair the meeting.

Sandra Lee (Director, London), Ashley Williams (Director, Kimberley), and Mamadou Konate (Director, Johannesburg) have kindly agreed to serve as peer reviewers.

Cordially,
Maria

Dears,

As you are aware, the ABC Mediation Committee is an internal conciliation forum of first resort for the resolution of conflicts submitted by employees alleging unfair treatment or violation of employment contract terms. Its decisions are not binding.

ABC Mediation Committee will be hosting an overview of the last year's factsheets. All employees are invited to virtually attend this event, which will take place Wednesday, 7 January 2020, from 2:00 pm – 3:30 pm European Central Time. The speakers are:

- Introductory Remarks – Jacques Riviere, Executive Secretary
- Case Review Presenter – Alison Rometty, Counsel,
- Commentator – David Cheng, Senior Counsel

If possible, we ask that you share the event with your colleagues.

Those connecting through internal streaming may use the following link: http://link

Otherwise, kindly find below the Skype instructions to connect remotely.

We hope you are able to attend!

Sincerely,
Tom

Dear Colleagues,

We look forward to receiving your comments on the attached package by the end of the day, Friday, December 12, 2019 ECT.

Comments may be addressed to the team copied in this email. They are seeking guidance on the following aspects:

1. Are the analytical foundations for the work solid?
2. Is the material in the document appropriately structured and accessibly written?
3. Does the project scaling plan appropriately reflect and incorporate lessons learned from the pilot stage?

MEET

4. Does the marketing plan adequately emphasize the links between pricing and segmentation, taking advantage of low hanging fruits?

5. Are the implementation arrangements and measures to coordinate project activities across various functions and cross-sectoral interests appropriately defined?

Following the efficient review process, an annotated agenda will be prepared by the project team and circulated before the meeting.

Kind regards,
Rebecca

⇒ Proposing the Time/Place for the Meeting

- 💬 Would half-past two suit you?
- 💬 How about next Monday at two?
- 💬 What time do you have in mind?
- 💬 Which day do you have in mind?
- 💬 How about sometime next week?

MEET

- What about this afternoon instead?
- Would you be available on Wednesday?
- Can I suggest that we meet at our offices?
- Are we going to meet the whole morning?
- Would Friday next week be suitable for you?
- Let say on the 1st of February in the morning.
- Could we perhaps meet next week to go over the details?
- Let's keep the length of the meeting to one hour for now.
- Let's say about one hour and a half. Is that all right for you?
- Would it be suitable to meet on June 10 at your Seattle offices to discuss?

⇒ When You Are Not Ok with the Appointment

- Sorry, I can't make it then.
- I'd love to, but I really can't.

MEET

- 💬 Sorry, I'm already tied up until two.
- 💬 I'm afraid I've got another meeting then.
- 💬 I am afraid I have another appointment then.
- 💬 I'm afraid we'll need to find another schedule.
- 💬 I'm afraid I can't meet them at ten next Monday.
- 💬 I'm afraid I can't make it next Friday. Why don't we put it off sometime next week?
- 💬 Unfortunately, I will be on a trip from January 3 to 8, so I couldn't make it then. Although, in the upcoming week, it will be a pleasure to meet with you.

⇒ **When You Are Ok with the Appointment**

In Speaking

- 💬 So, that's Monday at 10 AM.
- 💬 Yes, that's fine. See you then.
- 💬 Sounds Ok to me. Let's do that.

MEET

- Perfect, see you on Monday at 10.
- All right. I'll see you on Monday at 5:30.
- I look forward to seeing you on Tuesday.
- Well, this schedule suits me. Let's do that.
- I am looking forward to hearing from you.
- Excellent. I look forward to meeting you then.
- Perfect. I very much look forward to talking with you.
- That sounds sensible. So, I'll see you on Monday at 2.
- Yes, that would be fine. Let's say it's settled. See you then.
- All right, that's perfect for me. I look forward to meeting you.
- Yes, next week works fine. Shall we plan it at two on Monday?
- That would be just fine. I can't wait to meet you. See you on Monday.
- Just to confirm the schedule of our meeting: Tuesday 10 July at 10 AM.

In Writing

- Dear ...,

    Again, thank you for the email. I want to confirm my participation to the kickoff meeting on Friday, May 5, at the New York offices. If possible, I would like to have the risk analysis notes to get a head start.

    Yours truly,

MEET

📄 Dear ...,

This is to confirm my participation at the Review meeting on Monday, November 25, from 11:30 am to 1:00 pm UTC.

Thanks for sharing all the necessary documentation ahead of the meeting; this is appreciated.

Kindly book me a room in the same hotel and a rental car for in-city transportation.

Thanks for your world-class assistance,

Oliver

📄 Dear ...,

I am writing to confirm the meeting made over the phone yesterday. We agreed to meet at the Novotel Paris Centre on Thursday, June 7, at 10 am.

Please contact me at +33 xx-xxxxx or reply to this mail if there is any change of time or location. Feel free to call my assistant or me if you have any questions.

I look forward to meeting you.

Yours truly,

📄 Dear ...,

This is a gentle reminder to confirm your meeting with Eliyahu Goldman tomorrow January 22nd, by 11 am. He will meet you at your office.

Kindly reach out to me for any useful accommodation.

Thank you and have a fruitful meeting.

Respectfully,

⇒ Put off or Cancel

💬 I'm afraid our meeting is conflicting with another appointment I didn't consider. If you don't mind, I propose that we put it off. What about next Thursday at two?

💬 Could we put off our tomorrow meeting for I am not feeling good these days? I will need to rest tomorrow, as my doctor recommended. But if you don't mind, I am up for next Wednesday at nine at the same place.

💬 I am sorry to inform you that we will not be able to meet tomorrow. I got a last-minute change in a committee session. Please let me know if next Monday at ten will suit you. Otherwise, tell me when we could reschedule the rendezvous.

💬 An unexpected event just occurred, and as a result, I have to cancel our appointment. I know it's short notice and I'm sorry about that. I can't seem to find any spot in the coming days. But call me next week so that we can work something out.

⇒ Apologies

💬 I'm afraid I have an impediment that prevents me from attending the meeting. Just to inform you and present apologies.

💬 I'm afraid I've got an important and urgent engagement to handle. I will not be able to take part in the meeting. Wishing you a fruitful workshop.

💬 Unfortunately, I will not be able to attend the review meeting as a result of unforeseen events that cropped up. I am looking forward to reading the minutes to keep up with you. Have a productive and fruitful meeting.

❝ I'm afraid I have a critical project that is running late and needs my full attention. Hence, I will not be able to attend tomorrow's meeting. If you need any documentation from me, kindly let me know. Have a good day.

⇒ Follow Up

❝ My assistant will let you know the schedule of the meeting.

❝ My assistant will also be joining us. She will get in touch with you for all the details.

❝ I will have my assistant send you an email to let you know the time and place of our appointment.

❝ I will have my PA send you an email to let you know where our meeting will be held. She will also send you the agenda I'd like to discuss.

Open

⇒ Short Expressions to Open

💬 Good afternoon and welcome to this meeting. I will keep it as brief as possible since we are all busy these days. Can we make a start?

💬 Thanks for attending this important meeting. The discussions will be necessary to define a clear path for the new policy implementation. As all participants have received the documentation, let's go around the table to allow everyone to introduce himself.

💬 Good evening. Thanks for taking the time to have this meeting. We have called it to examine the business proposal of an information security startup. Let's go around the table for participants to introduce themselves. As everyone is here, let's begin.

💬 Good morning. Thanks for coming. We have a lot of ground to cover, so let's get started. Before going any further, I am pleased to introduce a new consultant, Mrs. Lynda Prayat. She will be working with the healthcare team. Welcome on board, Lynda! I wish you all the best in this new assignment. You have the floor.

💬 Thanks to all of you. We have a tight schedule today, so we'll need to cut corners. Let's get the ball rolling. But before, I have the privilege to introduce the new Digital Director, Mr. McMillan. He has a very long list of accomplishments in the sector, and many of us already met him on different occasions. Mr. McMillan, welcome on board! The floor is yours.

⇒ Informal Meeting at a Restaurant

Greetings

💬 Hello David, it's good to see you again.

Welcome to Hong Kong.

Thanks for arranging this informal meeting.

I hope you made a safe trip.

Did you have any trouble finding the place?

Did you find your way with no trouble?

Are you familiar with the area?

💬 Good afternoon Kim, it's always a pleasure meeting with you.

Thanks for taking the time to have this informal meeting.

I hope you made a safe commute.

Did you get the correct indications from the assistant?

How about your colleague Christopher at the Boston office?

💬 Hello Abdel, how have you been?

How is the family?

How about the traffic?

This restaurant is charming.

MEET

Thanks for taking the lead to have this meeting.

I hope you made safe travel.

Are you familiar with the area?

Which hotel are you staying?

How about your colleague Adams at the Boston office?

Did you get good indications from the assistant?

Opening Discussion (consulting request)

- What are you up to?
- Are you hitting the buffers?
- What can you tell me about your product?
- Where do you stand in your new software project?
- What is at the top of your agenda for this meeting?
- Are you also consulting with our so-called all-time competitors on other projects?
- It's in the air that your food-processing branch distribution system is facing aggressive competition.
- Are there specific objectives that the CEO of your firm wants to meet, and what is the dedicated timeframe on his agenda?

Opening Discussion (job request)

- Can you walk us through your CV?
- Can you tell me a bit about yourself?
- What do you know about our clients?

- What do you know about our market?
- What do you know about our products?
- How many cars were sold globally last year?
- Are you good at solving big hairy problems?
- What are some of your sectorial competences?
- Tell me about a time you changed someone's mind.
- What are your most robust functional competences?
- Can you tell me why you are interested in this position?
- Can you tell me about a significant personal achievement?
- "What important truth do very few people agree with you?" (2)
- Did you ever break the rules, and what are some of the cases?
- Are you well versed in financial legislation as required for the position?
- What is the biggest project problem you have solved, and how you made it?
- Give a case where you had an issue with your boss and the way it wound up.
- Are you good at managing teams remotely and handling multiple projects?
- What is your unique selling proposition for this position, or why should we hire you?
- Will you make it in the tech industry, and how are you planning to hit the ground running?
- Is there any particular reason why you are interested in changing companies at this moment?

💬 What means risk management for you, and can you give me a case where you mitigated a serious risk?

⇒ Formal Meetings

Greetings

💬 Hi everyone, welcome to this meeting.

💬 Dear participants, welcome to the 2nd review meeting of the year.

💬 Ladies and gentlemen welcome to the 2nd annual review meeting of the Southern American region's portfolio.

💬 Dear officials, representatives, investors, lenders, partners, managers, recipients, and actors welcome to this meeting.

Absence

💬 We have apologies from many stakeholders for today's meeting.

💬 Unfortunately, many are not able to make it today due to tight conflicting agendas.

💬 At least three persons are going to miss out on today's meeting due to conflicting schedules.

Context

💬 Since the last gathering, quite a few milestones have been covered.

💬 We have covered a pretty large amount of ground **since** the last review.

💬 **Since** the previous meeting, teams have worked hard, along with challenging changes in the environment.

- **During 2018**, we have initiated several organizational adjustments to enhance our ability to achieve better outcomes for our clients, and to strengthen our expertise and footprint on corporate strategy issues.
- **Following a year during which** we registered our weakest revenues performance of the past five years, sales growth is expected to slightly recover in 2019. However, the market is confronted by numerous risks, including exchange rates, financial stress, and geopolitical concerns.
- **By the end of this year**, it is estimated that a new regulation will be adopted by the Congress regarding food, beverage, and supplement labeling as well as ingredient review.

Objective / Agenda

- The task at the top of our agenda is the review of performance.
- We are here today because our new drug failed to get FDA approval.
- The main objective of the meeting is to go over the new risk mitigation plan.
- We'll be going through the report of the telecommunication authority, which is pretty bad.
- We'll be discussing the terms of reference for the upcoming international symposium in Italy.
- We'll be looking at the staff turnaround plan and discussing scenarios for overheads optimization.
- The objective of the meeting is to prepare the due diligence for the airline client's acquisition of *Fly the World*.
- The board had advanced the schedule for new projects' approval, so we will be working on nailing down all projects in the pipeline.

Box 1: 5 Rules to Be an Effective Team Player

1. Add value in meetings by getting your points across intelligently.

2. Make constructive criticism and help others also to get their points across.

3. Do your homework ahead of meetings by preparing your points along with relevant research.

4. Know your role in the meeting and play to that: support, evaluation, presentation, moderation, advice, or technical.

5. Listen actively, take notes, and show interest by closing your laptop and locking your smartphone.

Agree

exactly/ absolutely/ definitely	we are on the same page/ I adhere to	I fully agree with you/ of course/ sure	I couldn't agree more/ I perfectly agree
we are on the same wavelength	you took the words right out of my mouth	I couldn't say it any better	why not?/ agreed/ I have no objection
nothing to say/ Why not?	no doubt/ in the same vein/ furthermore	I share your point of view	this is also my point of view
I approve/ I also think that	I suppose so/ I guess so	I quite agree/ I totally agree/ I truly agree	I will just add that/ that's right
just to complete/ I also confirm	we agree with you/ we totally agree with	we acknowledge and agree that	we see eye to eye/ that's a good point

💬 I suppose so.

💬 Exactly. That's true.

💬 We are on the same page.

MEET

- 💬 I fully agree with you.
- 💬 I couldn't say it any better.
- 💬 I totally agree with Roberto.
- 💬 I share your point of view.
- 💬 This is also my point of view.
- 💬 Why not? I have no objection.
- 💬 We are on the same wavelength.
- 💬 I couldn't agree more on this point.
- 💬 No doubt, this proposition is the best.
- 💬 I also think that this is the right thing to do.
- 💬 You took the words right out of my mouth.
- 💬 I think we are now on the same wavelength.
- 💬 I will just add that we will even save more money.
- 💬 Feel free to agree or disagree and express your views.
- 💬 I also think that this level of overspending is a big issue.
- 💬 I also confirm that the project wasn't adequately funded.
- 💬 I am OK if you say that the vendor is competent for the job.
- 💬 In the same vein, I strongly agree with the low-cost proposition.
- 💬 I hope you agree with me that this is not the case for that client.
- 💬 The board will adhere to the restructuring plan if we present a forecasted scorecard.

- **I fully agree with you that** there is a need to strengthen the existing covenant provisions.

- **I agree with** Mrs. Aditya **on** this point that setting a high anchor price will help secure a better deal.

- **We acknowledge and agree that** we have not entered a contractual relationship with the supplier regarding such a bundle offer.

- **We agree with you,** Mr. Chairman, **and with you,** Mr. Director, that the firm, and more particularly the IT department, can enhance its capacity to handle the software configuration.

MEET

Disagree

I'm afraid I don't agree with	I tend to disagree with	you may not even agree with me	I don't share your point of view
forget it/ you must be joking	I take your point/ it's too risky	I don't think it's a good idea	I don't know/ it's a long shot
I strongly disagree	absolutely not/ of course not	nothing of the kind	sorry, but .../ excuse me, but ...
there is a problem with	it's looks good on paper, but ...	I am not sure I agree with you	It's true, but ...

- To be honest, **I don't think it's a good idea**.
- **It's true, but** only for one region out five regions surveyed.
- **I'm afraid** this strategy will reveal some of our weaknesses.
- **I tend to disagree** with any kind of ill-informed decision-making.
- **You may not even agree with me**, but this little app is the solution.
- **Of course not**, we are not saying that your team is not competent.
- **I strongly disagree** with the proposition to force the hand of the union.

- 💬 **It looks good on paper, but** it's going to be an uphill battle to execute.

- 💬 **I'm afraid I don't agree** with you on the composition of the negotiating team.

- 💬 **I am not sure I agree with you** on this work plan, especially on the first-round activities.

- 💬 **I don't think it is a good idea to** target 4% market share in only a three-year time frame.

- 💬 **It is too risky** to put all the eggs in one basket, especially when it comes to Forex trading.

- 💬 **There is a problem with** this proposition because we don't have the results of the survey yet.

- 💬 **This option is a long shot** because it is unlikely that you will educate people to create a market for your product.

MEET

Interrupt

sorry for interrupting you, but ...	let's get back on track	I apologize for interrupting, but ...	I'm afraid I have to interrupt you
we'll take that up later	we'll come back to you in a second	you will get a spot to share your view	you will have the opportunity to react
can I just interrupt you here?	can we go back to ...	please, let's hear what [ ] has to say	could I finish please?
let's close this parenthesis	let's hit a pause	hold on a moment please	can I come in here?
if I could just come in here	could I just say something about that?	just a second please, we'll get back to you.	let's get down to business

99 Let's get back on track.

99 If I could just come in here?

99 Can I just interrupt you here?

99 Could I finish, please? Thank you.

- 💬 We'll **come back** to you in a second.

- 💬 **Could I just say** something about that?

- 💬 Please, can we **go back to the point**?

- 💬 Just a **second**, please. We'll **get back** to you.

- 💬 Please, let's hear what Mrs. Sullivan has to say.

- 💬 **Let's** close this parenthesis and get back to the issue.

- 💬 **You will get a spot to speak** in a minute. Thank you.

- 💬 **Let's hit a pause.** We will get back after the coffee break.

- 💬 **Sorry for interrupting you**, but we must **get back on track**.

- 💬 **Hold** on a moment please, you will have a spot very soon.

- 💬 **I apologize for interrupting**, but we just need to know if there is a solution.

- 💬 Please, in a moment, **you will have the opportunity to share your views**. Thanks for your understanding.

- 💬 **I'm afraid I have to interrupt you** because the question is whether or not we can outsource the customer service and what the cost will be.

Ask Opinion

can you share your view about ...?	can you give your take on ..?	what's your opinion (advice) about ...?	do you think this idea has legs?
how do you anticipate ...?	how are you envisioning ...?	what do you think about ...?	would you like to share your opinion?
do you have any objection on ...?	can you share your thoughts on ...?	could you weigh in with your arguments?	how serious do you think it is?

💬 **What's your advice** on the sales targets?

💬 **Can you give your take** on this proposition?

💬 **Do you think** it will work in the Asian region?

💬 How important **do you think** the damages are?

💬 **How are you envisioning** the physical relocation of the factory?

💬 **What do you think about** the acquisition in terms of synergies?

💬 **How do you anticipate** problems in the delivery of a building permit?

💬 **Can you share your thoughts** on the performance of robots in your plant?

💬 **Do you have any objection** to the new management remuneration proposition?

💬 **Do you think it's a good idea** to link partners' remuneration to the performance of the fund?

💬 **Would you like to share your opinion** on the integration of the siloed systems into a unique platform?

MEET

Clarify

do you mean that ...?	are you saying that ...?	is your point that ...?	what I meant to say was ...
that's not what I meant	I was trying to say that ...	I'm afraid I didn't get you	it's worth mentioning that
can you put it in layman terms	it is important to mention that ...	the rationale of ... is that ...	there is a little misunderstanding here
I don't think you understood me well	I just want to highlight some of ...	It would be good to clarify that ...	don't get me wrong, I didn't say that

💬 That's not what I meant.

💬 I'm afraid I didn't get you.

💬 I think you heard me wrong.

💬 Don't get me wrong. I didn't say that.

💬 I don't think you understood me well.

💬 There is a little misunderstanding here.

💬 Are you saying that the prototype is not fully functional?

💬 There's a persistent misunderstanding about outsourcing.

- 💬 **Is your point that** the product launch should be postponed?
- 💬 **Would you like to explain** the agile meetings concept briefly?
- 💬 **I don't think you've well understood** the point of Mrs. Lopez.
- 💬 **I'm not sure I understand** you when saying fixed costs will vary.
- 💬 **I just want to highlight** the fact that costs will outweigh the benefits.
- 💬 **What I meant to say was** we must first focus on low hanging fruits.
- 💬 **Do you mean that** sales will decline as a result of the new legislation?
- 💬 **Please, can you put it in layman terms** so that everyone can follow up?
- 💬 **What I meant to say was** if there is no competition, there is no market.
- 💬 **I just want to highlight some of** the possibilities available in the short term.
- 💬 **I just wanted to highlight some** updates just in case it got buried in your mails.
- 💬 **I was trying to say that** over-communication is better than under-communication.
- 💬 **It would be good to clarify what** sunk costs are and that they are not considered in the net present value of the project.
- 💬 **It is important to mention that** partnership and proprietorship forms are not suitable for a startup expecting to raise funds and be sold in the future.
- 💬 **The rationale of** the $20 billion market size **is that** if a startup is successful and able to capture 5% of the market, then it could reach an income target of $1 billion per year.

Make a Point

here's the deal	the point is	I'd like to make a point here	if I could just add a point
I'd like to make a contribution	I'd like to draw your attention on	I'd like to warn you against	I want to emphasize that
I'd like to react to …	I'd like to highlight that	I'd like to add that …	I want to underscore that
in the same vein/ in the same way	just to make a small contribution…	I want to comment on …	could I draw your attention to …
could I come here?	can I make a point on …?	can I just comment on …?	could I bring a point on …?

💬 I'd like to comment on the product-market fit.

💬 The point is that it's not the hard part of the job.

💬 Could I just add a point here about the cost centers?

💬 Can I make a point here about Mr. Riley's intervention?

💬 This story makes very good points about people. Don't you agree?

MEET

- **Can I come here** to talk about the adoption strategy of the product?
- **I would like to make a point** about the positioning of the company.
- **The point is** the negotiation is much more complicated than expected.
- **If I could just add a point,** I want to explain the tests and measurements.
- **I want to emphasize that** the team must sign a non-disclosure agreement.
- **I would like to react to** Alan's presentation of the MVP (minimum viable product).
- **I'd like to shed light on** the conclusions of the team on the market validation.
- **I'd like to warn you against** the possible retaliation from foreign governments.
- **I'd like to draw your attention to** the software's end-user configuration requirements.
- **In the same vein,** higher customer service will also impact sales positively in the medium term.
- **Here's the deal:** the client moved up the deadline, so I need to see the draft as soon as possible.
- **In the same vein,** I want to add that the results of the customer survey are satisfactory if not perfect.
- **Just to make a small contribution,** I'd like to say that the accuracy of the disbursement rate must be verified.

Give a Reason

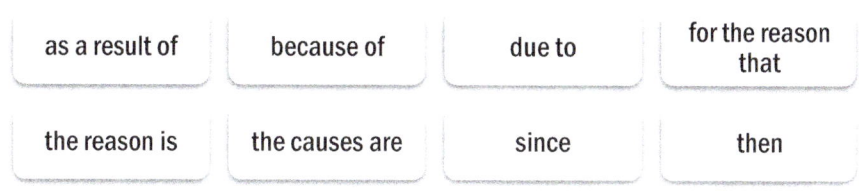

as a result of	because of	due to	for the reason that
the reason is	the causes are	since	then

💬 The budget overrun is **due to** poor general expenses forecasts.

💬 Higher margins, **as a result of** reduced prime costs may be expected.

💬 We are looking for a new designer **because** the current one is resigning.

💬 The region is still depressed **because of** criminality and low public investments.

💬 The new prototype seems to be a success **since** we got past all the preliminary tests.

💬 Costs are down here **for the reason** that the turnaround has reduced overhead expenses.

- **As a result of** the marketing campaign, revenue, and gross margin are higher than forecasted.
- The excellent usage rate of solar pumps is **due to** the massive implication of stakeholders.
- The services that we provide may become temporarily unavailable **as a result of** a system malfunction.
- We have not renewed the contract with the vendor. **The reason was** we were unhappy with their performance.
- Our customer base has grown by 6,500 in size between 2015 and 2017 **as a result of** higher market penetration.
- The conference was attended by a large public **as a result of** the excellent communication done by the PR department.
- Staff turnover, lack of funding, and burnout **are** some of **the primary causes** of the project's failure following implementation.
- On the Fintech Project, we need people with scientific backgrounds **because** it makes it much easier for the team to talk to one another.

Report Progress

- We were afraid the deal was lost, but our negotiation team **pulled a rabbit out of his hat** to get an agreement.
- We started this project on a shoestring, but the teams worked really hard **to scale it up into** a sizeable profitable venture.
- Months after searching how to boost declining market share, our company can now **get** an offensive strategy **off the ground**.

- 💬 Starting out in the grain business in 2011, our London-based subsidiary **had gradually expanded** into the food-processing industry.
- 💬 Since its inception in 2012 as a small development organization with a dozen employees in Bangalore, Water Project **had grown into** an internationally recognized, nonprofit social enterprise.

Report Regress

- 💬 Profits **have been declining over** the past three years.
- 💬 Local sales **have been declining over** the past two years.
- 💬 I am not responsible for the **mess**; you need to look somewhere else.
- 💬 The project **is going down in flames** due to siloed platforms failing to integrate.
- 💬 In the last quarter, the **profits were 15% lower than** the same quarter three years earlier.
- 💬 The new product launch **wasn't successful**, so all the hard work **went down the drain**.
- 💬 What can we do the reverse this trend of **declining profitability** in the premium market?
- 💬 Despite offering a high-end product, the company **fails to capture a fair share** of the premium market.
- 💬 The project on health care **wasn't approved** by the committee, so we have to go **back to the drawing board**.
- 💬 Unfortunately, the new tech venture **is not going to fly** due to **severe technical issues** to fill its central promise profitably.

> I don't want to **add fuel to the fire**, but the IT project **is also suffering** from the poor asset management of the administration team.

> Despite their unique brand name, the profits **dwindled significantly over** the past three years, and specifically in the previous quarter, net income **was down** 15% **compared to** last year.

Moderate

> **We can take that up later.** Let's focus on the task in hand.

> **We can take that up next week** at the staff meeting. **Let's get back to** the subject.

> **So far**, we have done a review of last month's activities. **Now we are going to make** the next month's agenda.

> **So far**, we have gathered insights into the new marketing plan. **Now I'd like to hit the next point.** Can you present the budgeted sales for next year?

> **We all agree,** to some extent, **that** ideas are irrelevant if there are not backed up with a minimum of data. **Now let's get to** the next point. What is the proposed team for the BIONADE engagement?

Close

> It was a very constructive meeting. Thanks for your participation. I wish you a fruitful day.

> Thanks for attending this workshop. The date of the next discussions will be communicated later. The meeting is over. Have a good day!

MEET

💬 The next meeting will take place in two weeks. Thanks for your active participation. The workshop is over. I wish you a productive day.

Case 1: Internal Meeting Transcript

[Chairman]: Good morning, everyone. I see empty chairs. Please, move closer to fill these places. We are required to make meetings agile, so this is going to be a 30-minute meeting.

Can we make a start? All right. Thank you all for coming despite the short notice. It's great seeing you all attend the meeting. I appreciate it. We didn't meet for four weeks, so there is a pretty large amount of ground to cover. We'll need to cut corners to make it in half an hour, so please be short and concise.

Before going further, let's go around the table to allow old and new participants to get to know each other.

Well, thanks. The proposed agenda is:

1. Apologies
2. Compliance and regulatory matters
3. Due diligence for *Fly The World* acquisition
4. Adoption of the human resource integration plan

Do we have excuses for today's meeting?

> [Catherine]: Pierre will come to the meeting late. Mary has informed that she is not going to attend this session. We have also received the apologies of Samantha because she is grappling with the labor union unrest.

[Chairman]: Good. Is there any amendment of agenda that someone would like to suggest?

> [David]: Thank you, John (chairman). I'd like to suggest that we put point 3 at the top of the agenda because the discussions will bring clarification for the second point.

[Jerry]: I wonder if it's not better to merge the third point on regulatory matters with the following point on due diligence because there is a redundancy.

[Ayush]: AOB (Any Other Business) is missing; it is useful for discussing miscellaneous issues that will come down the road.

[Chairman]: Ok, sounds good to me. So, please add to the minutes that the proposed amendments are applied. All right, let's get started.

[Chairman]: David, can you tell us where we stand on the acquisition of *Fly The World?*

[David]: Thanks, John. We had already informed the target that we own more than 15% of voting rights. I will let Jerry walk you through the due diligence checklist.

[Jerry]: Thank you. Here is the nine-point checklist of the due diligence.

- Corporate structure & general matters
- Taxes
- Strategic fit
- Intellectual property
- Material Assets
- Contracts
- Employees and senior management
- Litigation
- Compliance and regulatory matters

We have a couple of issues with taxes, intellectual property, and employees. These issues are related to the fact that a new piece of legislation is allegedly underway. It can hypothetically affect these elements. Otherwise, everything is under control.

[Chairman]: So, we are going to keep tabs on this legislation. We'll take that up next month to see how things are unfolding. Let's hit the next point. Can you present the plan for the integration of both companies' staff after acquisition?

> [Jerry]: As the companies are operating in the same industry industries, the priority will be to cut redundant senior positions. Therefore, C-level management will be drastically downsized for these positions will be attributed to the parent company's C-level. As a result, we are going to make 17 positions redundant at the C-level. Similarly, the business and operations levels will be trimmed to eliminate overstaffing. At these levels, 158 jobs are on the line. In summary, 175 positions will be stripped away.

[Chairman]: Thanks Jerry, for these efficient answers. I want you to pay close attention to labor unions. You might have to negotiate this plan and leave more jobs on the table. Please, follow this through very carefully and report directly to me. Don't surprise me because I hate surprises.

Do we have any other business?

...

Well, the next meeting will take place in two weeks. Thanks for your active participation. The meeting is over. I wish you a fruitful day.

Exercises

1. How would you call the meetings with the below information, in speaking and in writing?
    a. Date: Monday, January 20ᵗʰ 2020; time: 10 AM; place: Palace Restaurant; object: discuss a contract.
    b. Date: next week; time: 2 PM; place: office; object: prepare a mission.

2. Which are the five expressions used when you agree with someone?
    a. We are on the same page
    b. Sorry for interrupting you, but
    c. I quite agree
    d. Is your point that ...?
    e. I agree with you
    f. I couldn't say it any better
    g. I'd like to react to
    h. I take your point
    i. It is important to mention that
    j. We are on the same wavelength
    k. I tend to disagree with you

3. Which are the three expressions that are not used to make a point?
    a. I'd like to make a point here
    b. Could I finish please?
    c. If I could just add a point
    d. I take your point
    e. I'd like to make a contribution
    f. I'd like to draw your attention on
    g. I'd like to warn you about
    h. I'm afraid I don't agree with you
    i. I want to emphasize that

Chapter 2
TALK

Some people just speak, while others consistently compile a code of thinking.

Greet Differently

⇒ **Say Hello**

hi there	hello there	hi champion	how is life?	what's new?
how do you do?	how is it going?	hope all is well	hope you are well and safe	it's been a while
it's good to see you	it's nice to meet you	how are things?	how is everything?	what's going on?
how are you doing?	how have you been?	how are you feeling?	how is your day?	how is your day going?
how is the family?	how are the kids?	long time no see	what's good?	hope all is good with you
how is it going today?	how's this day working out?	how have you been since last time?	how have you been lately?	what have you been up to?
how are things with you?	what's up? *(informal)*	how you feeling? *(informal)*	how you doing? *(informal)*	howdy/ you alright? *(informal)*

⇒ Reply to Hello

I'm fine/ just fine	I'm very well	I'm super well	very well, thanks	I'm going well
I'm good/ I'm pretty good	good/ pretty good	going well/ going great	I'm going great	I'm on a great form
I feel on top of the world	I couldn't feel better!	I'm terrific!/ I'm fired up!	I'm fully charged!	battery is full!
incredibly good looking	I am blessed!	so far, so good!	I think I'm doing okay	oh, busy as usual
I'm doing really well	new day, same things	just the same old	oh, just the usual	busy as ever, but I'll survive
I've been better	better than some days	I've seen better days	I'm vertical and breathing	I'm hanging in there
really good, thanks for asking	having the time of my life	sunshine all day long!	the best I can be, assuming you too!	way better than I deserve!
happy and content, thank you	still on caffeine, as usual	dreaming about vacation	medium well/ not so well	it's the status quo out there
not too bad/ I'm not too bad	I'm vertical	nothing much/ not fiesta	I'm feeling down	I'm not good today
much better now that you called	I would be lying if I said I'm good	I'm still alive/ surviving, I guess	I'm pretty standard right now	I have a pulse, so I must be okay

TALK

⇒ Say Goodbye

hello there	bye	bye-bye	goodbye	bye for now
ciao	cheers	ta-ta	so long	see you
see you soon	see you later	farewell	Gob bless!	take care
good night	keep fit	salaam	all the best	good night
good day	bye for now	see you soon	stay safe	stay well
see you tomorrow	aurevoir	arrivederci	sayonara	adios
auf wiedersehen	good afternoon	good morning	have a nice day	catch you later
catch you later	have a great day	talk to you later	I'll be seeing you	mind how you go
nice to see you	hope we meet again	it was nice to talk to you	look after yourself	it's been a pleasure to …

⇒ When a Colleague Is Sick

get well soon!	recover soon!	feel better soon!	praying for recovery
get well very quickly!	sending hugs and love!	have a quick recovery!	have a speedy recovery!
wish you a fast recovery	hope you feel better soon	return to full health soon!	wish you a speedy recovery

hope you have a swift recovery	hoping for your speedy recovery	hoping for a smooth recovery	sending you healing thoughts
wish you a quick return to health	you will be healthy and smiling again	sending good, healthy vibes your way	hope you feel a little better every day
hang in there. Better days are coming	looking forward to seeing you healthy	we're all wishing you a speedy recovery	hoping you find strength with each new day

- 💬 Wish you a fast recovery.
- 💬 Hope you feel better soon.
- 💬 Return to full health soon!
- 💬 Wish you a speedy recovery.
- 💬 Hoping for a smooth recovery.
- 💬 Sending you healing thoughts.
- 💬 Hope you have a swift recovery.
- 💬 Hoping for your speedy recovery.
- 💬 Wish you a quick return to health.
- 💬 You will be healthy and smiling again.
- 💬 Sending good, healthy vibes your way.
- 💬 Hope you feel a little better every day.
- 💬 Hang in there. Better days are coming!
- 💬 Looking forward to seeing you healthy.
- 💬 We're all wishing you a speedy recovery.
- 💬 Hoping you find strength with each new day.

Express Gratitude Differently

⇒ Thank You

thanks for your time	thank you so much	thank you so very much	you made my day	I appreciate your time
It's really appreciated	I owe you one	I'm so thankful	I'm truly grateful	I'm so touched
I'll pay you back	you're awesome	you're the best!	you're amazing	you saved my life
you're a lifesaver	you're too kind	you're so thoughtful	you're so generous	that's so kind of you
I appreciate your support	you know how to make me happy	thanks for this, you've read in my mind	I appreciate your suggestion	thanks for your collaboration
I'm thankful for your partnership	I'm grateful for your friendship	thanks for your prompt action	thanks for your assistance	thank you for letting me know
thanks for getting back to me	I'm grateful for your gesture	thanks for responding quickly	thanks for your comments	what would I do without you?

thanks for your fortitude	you didn't need to do that	you've gone above and beyond	I feel blessed to have such a team	that means so much to me
I couldn't have done it without you	I will never forget	thanks for your commitment and dedication	I'm truly reconnassant	thanks for your help

- Thanks for buying the book :)
- Thanks for this. Appreciated.
- Thanks for the input. Appreciated.
- Thank you. I really needed a coffee.
- Thank You, Chris. You made my day.
- Thank you, Sammy. It's very kind of you.
- You're the best Subra! You save my life.
- What a thoughtful gift. I really appreciate it!
- Thank you so much. You shouldn't have.
- I don't know what to say! That's very kind.
- Thanks for anticipating this. You're the best.
- You're awesome! Thanks for your assistance.
- I feel blessed to have such an incredible team!
- Thanks for the coffee, you've read in my mind.
- Thanks a lot for the present. I really appreciate it.
- Thanks a bunch for this opportunity. You saved my life.
- You're the best. We wouldn't close the deal without you.

TALK

💬 Thanks a bunch. I really appreciate it. You made my day.

💬 Looking forward to your response. Thanks for your time.

💬 All I can say is thank you. I am speechless! This is fantastic!

💬 Thanks for these perfect PowerPoint lessons. I owe you one.

💬 Thanks, Abdel. Wonderful exchanging while you were there!

💬 Thanks for the donuts. You really know how to make me happy.

💬 I really owe you one. Thanks for your support. The next time you need help, I've got it.

💬 We want to thank all employees for their continuing fortitude a determination amidst this uncertainty.

⇒ You're Welcome

it's all good	my pleasure	anytime	no big deal
no problem	no worries	same to you	with pleasure
you got it	you're most welcome	you're quite welcome	you're truly welcome
you're very welcome	don't mention it	no need to thank me	don't worry about it
it's/it was nothing	it's/it was not a big deal	glad I could help	glad I could give a hand
it's/it was the least I could do	it's/it wasn't a problem for me	anything to make you happy	I know you would do the same for me

TALK

- 💬 You're very welcome.
- 💬 You're truly welcome.
- 💬 You're most welcome.
- 💬 You're quite welcome.
- 💬 No worries. You got it.
- 💬 Anytime, with pleasure.
- 💬 Glad I could give a hand.
- 💬 It's nothing. My pleasure.
- 💬 It was the least I could do.
- 💬 No problem. It was nothing.
- 💬 Glad I could help. Anytime.
- 💬 Anything to make you happy.
- 💬 No big deal. You're welcome.
- 💬 It's all good. Don't mention it.
- 💬 You got it. Don't worry about it.
- 💬 Don't mention it. It was nothing.
- 💬 It wasn't a problem for me. You got it.
- 💬 I know you would do the same for me.
- 💬 It was the least I could do. No big deal.
- 💬 It's no big deal. Just my way to give back.
- 💬 No need to thank me. Glad I could help.
- 💬 No big deal. I know you would do the same for me.

Diversify Your English

Below are some of the best tips to enhance your speaking to sound more professional. Kindly note that these are *not* perfect synonyms, but in most cases, you can alternate between them without affecting the meaning of your ideas.

Alternate this	⇔	With that
A few	⇔	A couple of
A little	⇔	Slightly
Advanced	⇔	Cutting-edge/ state-of-the-art
After	⇔	Afterward
Almost	⇔	Just about
Also	⇔	As well *(end of clause)*
Approximately	⇔	Roughly/ to the tune of/ around/ about
Ask *(verb)*	⇔	Question/ demand/ request/ inquire *(verb)*
At all levels	⇔	Across the board
At the end	⇔	At the end of the day

TALK

At-risk	⇔	On the line/ at stake
Attractive	⇔	Gorgeous
Avoid *(verb)*	⇔	Shy away/ steer clear from *(verb)*
Bad luck	⇔	Misfortune
Basically	⇔	Roughly
Be able to *(verb)*	⇔	Be capable of *(verb)*
Be between *(verb)*	⇔	Range across/ range between *(verb)*
Be good at *(verb)*	⇔	Have a knack for/ have a gift for *(verb)*
Be in charge *(verb)*	⇔	Oversee *(verb)*
Be lucky *(verb)*	⇔	Have good fortune *(verb)*
Be working *(verb)*	⇔	Be on the ball *(verb)*
Before	⇔	Prior to/ ahead of
Be late *(verb)*	⇔	Run late *(verb)*
Cause *(verb)*	⇔	Result in *(verb)*
Cause problems *(verb)*	⇔	Raise issues/ raise concerns/ give rise to problems *(verb)*
Chance/ luck	⇔	Fortune
Change *(verb)*	⇔	Shift/ pivot *(verb)*
Check *(verb)*	⇔	Kick the tires *(verb)*
Common	⇔	Ubiquitous
Concern *(verb)*	⇔	Relate to/ be linked to *(verb)*
Concerning/ about	⇔	Regarding/ with regard to/ with respect to
Conclusion	⇔	Bottom line
Contact *(verb)*	⇔	Reach out to/ get in touch *(verb)*
Context	⇔	Backdrop
Continue *(verb)*	⇔	Keep going *(verb)*
Contribute *(verb)*	⇔	Bring to the table *(verb)*

TALK

Copy someone *(email)*	⇌	Loop in *(verb)*
Cover *(verb)*	⇌	Cut across/ cut through *(verb)*
Danger	⇌	Common pitfall/ trap/ risk
Despite	⇌	At the expense of
Destined to fail	⇌	Doomed to fail/ bound to fail
Dishonest	⇌	Shady/ questionable
Detail	⇌	Nitty-gritty
During	⇌	Along with/ along the way
Easy	⇌	A breeze/ a piece of cake
Easy success	⇌	Home run
Exceed limit *(verb)*	⇌	Overrun *(verb)*
Encounter *(verb)*	⇌	Come across *(verb)*
Enough	⇌	Pretty/ quite
Ephemeral	⇌	Short-lived
Equally	⇌	Evenly
Escape *(verb)*	⇌	Ride out/ get off the hook *(verb)*
Estimate	⇌	Proxy
Existing company	⇌	Incumbent company
Expand *(verb)*	⇌	Scale up *(verb)*
Fail *(verb)*	⇌	Fall through *(verb)*
Finish *(verb)*	⇌	End/ Come to an end/ Be over/ Complete *(verb)*
For example	⇌	For instance/ as an example/ say
Freedom of action	⇌	Leeway
From nowhere	⇌	Out of the blue
From X to Y	⇌	From X all the way up to Y/ From X all the way down to Y
Get *(verb)*	⇌	Obtain/ acquire/ receive *(verb)*
Give *(verb)*	⇌	Provide *(verb)*

Give up *(verb)*	⇔	Abandon *(verb)*
Give your opinion *(verb)*	⇔	Share your view/ give your take/ give your standpoint *(verb)*
Go bankrupt *(verb)*	⇔	Go belly up *(verb)*
Good job!	⇔	Way to go!
Happening	⇔	Underway/ occurring
Have bad luck *(verb)*	⇔	Have misfortune *(verb)*
Have problems *(verb)*	⇔	Be in trouble *(verb)*
Highlight *(verb)*	⇔	Play up *(verb)*
Identify *(verb)*	⇔	Pinpoint *(verb)*
Ignore *(verb)*	⇔	Lose sight of *(verb)*
Important	⇔	Essential/sizeable/major/critical/ dominant/substantial/considerable
In fact	⇔	Actually/ as a matter of fact
In general	⇔	Typically/ generally speaking
In order to	⇔	As a way of/ as a way to
In serious difficulty	⇔	In dire straits/ in trouble/ in a tight corner
Inactive	⇔	Sluggish
Irrational	⇔	Delusional
It can be said that	⇔	Arguably/ one can argue that
It looks like	⇔	It seems to be
It's a good idea	⇔	It makes sense/ the idea has legs
It's not certain	⇔	There is a long way to go/ it's not given/ it's not self-evident
It sounds good	⇔	It makes sense/ it looks really good/ it sounds great
It's uncertain	⇔	It's a long shot
Jump *(verb)*	⇔	Leapfrog *(verb)*
Last	⇔	Previous/ former/ recent

TALK

Large quantity	⇔	A great deal of (uncountable)/ sizeable/ massive/ huge
Later	⇔	Down the line/ down the road
Lead to development *(verb)*	⇔	Drive development *(verb)*
Lead to growth *(verb)*	⇔	Drive growth *(verb)*
Lead to innovation *(verb)*	⇔	Drive innovation *(verb)*
Lead to progress *(verb)*	⇔	Drive progress *(verb)*
Let them know *(verb)*	⇔	Inform *(verb)*
Lie *(verb)*	⇔	Make stuff up/ tell fibs *(verb)*
Make progress *(verb)*	⇔	Come a long way *(verb)*
Many types of	⇔	Wide range of/ broad range of/ wide array of
Many/ a lot of/ several	⇔	Quite a few/plenty of/a bunch of
Maybe	⇔	Hypothetically/ probably
Motivation	⇔	Drive/ momentum/ impetus
Next	⇔	Ahead *(after the noun)*/ to come *(after the noun)*/ upcoming
No matter	⇔	Regardless of
No one	⇔	None of us/ none of them
Normally	⇔	Typically
Not at all	⇔	By no means/ whatsoever
On my side	⇔	From my end
Oppose *(verb)*	⇔	Be up against *(verb)*
Out of danger	⇔	Out of trouble/ out of the hoods/ off the hook
Overspending	⇔	Budget overrun
Pass/ traverse *(verb)*	⇔	Get past/ get through *(verb)*
Persist *(verb)*	⇔	Prevail/ carry on *(verb)*

TALK

Prevent/ disturb *(verb)*	⇔	Get in the way/ stand in the way *(verb)*
Produce *(verb)*	⇔	Generate *(verb)*
Provoke *(verb)*	⇔	Trigger/ activate *(verb)*
Reject *(verb)*	⇔	Dismiss *(verb)*
Remind *(verb)*	⇔	Recall *(verb)*
Remove *(verb)*	⇔	Strip away *(verb)*
Retire *(verb)*	⇔	Pull out *(verb)*
Say differently *(verb)*	⇔	Put differently *(verb)*
Schedule	⇔	Agenda
Search an example *(verb)*	⇔	Look for an analogy *(verb)*
Simply	⇔	Roughly/ basically
Simply said *(verb)*	⇔	Simply stated *(verb)*
Small/ insignificant	⇔	Trivial
Solve *(verb)*	⇔	Deal with/ cope with/ handle/ grapple with/ get to grips with *(verb)*
Solution	⇔	Way out
Some	⇔	Some of
Standard/ universal	⇔	One-size-fits-all
Start quickly *(verb)*	⇔	Dive in/ jump in *(verb)*
Stay neutral *(verb)*	⇔	Sit on the fence *(verb)*
Succeed *(verb)*	⇔	Make it *(verb)*
Successively	⇔	In a row
Suddenly	⇔	All of a sudden
Strange	⇔	Peculiar
Take a risk *(verb)*	⇔	Take a chance *(verb)*
Take it personally *(verb)*	⇔	Make things personal *(verb)*
Talk about *(verb)*	⇔	Discuss/ exchange on *(verb)*
Tell why *(verb)*	⇔	Give reasons/give explanations *(verb)*

TALK

Then/ therefore	⇌	As a result
Think about (verb)	⇌	Reflect upon/ reflect on (verb)
Think the same (verb)	⇌	Feel the same (verb)
Thus/ therefore	⇌	Whereby
Transform into (verb)	⇌	Turn into (verb)
Understand (verb)	⇌	Figure out/ grasp/ pick up (verb)
Unregulated	⇌	Unchartered
Use (verb)	⇌	Leverage/ tap into/ exploit (verb)
Wait for (verb)	⇌	Look forward (verb)
Well done!	⇌	Way to go!
Weird	⇌	Peculiar
Will not happen (verb)	⇌	Is not going to happen (verb)
Without success	⇌	To no avail

⇒ Rewritten Phrases

💬 I'd like to make (a few) a couple of observations.

💬 I believe we'll find (a solution) a way out very quickly.

💬 Shortly (after) afterward, we'll have a meeting with a client.

💬 Natural gas is (a little) slightly more expensive than gasoline.

💬 The company (went bankrupt) went belly up only after two years.

💬 It's an excellent opportunity, but there are (also) some risks as well.

💬 There is no (standard) one-size-fits-all solution for this kind of problem.

💬 This procedure usually takes from a few hours to (a few) a couple of days.

- Some of the (~~Some~~) candidates have demonstrated strong analytical skills.

- This event is too (~~insignificant~~) **trivial** to (~~provoke~~) **trigger** a military attack.

- Can you (~~tell why there are delivery delays~~) **give the reasons for** delivery delays?

- Teams worked hard to scale it up into a (~~large~~) **sizeable** profitable venture.

- This vendor can provide (~~almost~~) **just about** any electronic device for the office.

- The amount of the economic stimulus is (~~approximately~~) **to the tune of** $1 trillion.

- Fifty years back, these ideas seemed impossible to (~~transform into~~) **turn into** reality.

- We need to (~~understand~~) **figure out** why they decided to end the partnership.

- (~~Take a risk~~) **Take a chance** on the new treatment. It might be the end of your health troubles.

- In today's meeting, we will (~~talk about~~) **discuss** the implementation of the new operations policy.

- A government-appointed mediator has tried to move talks forward, but (~~without success~~) **to no avail**.

- The platform would also give managers the ability to share information and (~~use~~) **leverage** resources.

- This is (~~not at all~~) **by no means** an exhaustive list of targets, but only a quick selection to show possibilities.

TALK

- There is no (~~unregulated~~) **unchartered** market in the economy unless it is very trivial and harmless for people.

- My field of competence (~~covers~~) **cuts across** artificial intelligence, programming, and data management.

- The proposal they have made is not satisfactory and (~~therefore~~), as a result, we have taken the case to court.

- The reality is that such an innovation (~~will not happen~~) **is not going to happen** without (~~many~~) **a great deal of** failure.

- This situation (~~causes some problems~~) **gives rise to concerns** that the unintended downstream effects will be even worse.

- Therefore, our team will (~~think about~~) **reflect upon** additional measures, including, but not limited to incentive schemes.

- The NAFTA report (~~identified~~) **pinpointed** several consequences for the U.S. economy if the agreement is (~~retired~~) **pulled out**.

- The multinational company has recently applied a new medical benefits plan (~~at all levels~~) **across the board** to stay attractive.

- Meetings will be held on a weekly basis (~~to talk about~~) **to exchange on** progress and possible difficulties faced during the implementation of the program.

Make Great Conversations

⇒ **Conditional Expressions**

I wish

💬 **I wish I had** a better memory for people's names.

💬 **I wish I had** asked myself when I was in grad school.

💬 **I wish we took** a coffee break before moving forward.

💬 **I wish it were** the other scenario, which is less expensive.

💬 **I wish I were** there to defend myself against these allegations.

💬 **I wish he were** more friendly and open-minded as a colleague.

If/ as if

💬 He acts **as if he were** the supervisor.

💬 I wouldn't worry about it **if I were** you.

💬 I would have accepted to transfer to Asia **if I had** no kid.

💬 It's not **as if I were** not interested. It's just not the right time.

TALK

- **If he were** not so hard-working, he wouldn't make it to partner.
- You must think **as if you were** the CEO to capture the big picture.
- **If I were** the CEO, I would have this guy promoted to branch manager.

Had that been

- **Had that been** the case, we would have lost the contract.
- **Had that been** today, I would have done things differently.
- **Had that been** the case, a binding agreement wouldn't have seen the light of day.
- **Had that been** Oliver, we wouldn't have bothered making a trip to monitor the task.

That

- I recommend **that you be** more open to your team.
- We requested **that the office not be** locked at weekends.
- The client demanded **that you be** in the engagement team.
- We proposed **that the company focus** on untapped segments.
- The union is keen **that employees not be** laid off after the merger.
- It was essential **that the company implement** recommendations rapidly.

Suppose

- **Suppose** the client firm were here. What would you ask them?

💬 **Suppose you had** no information. What recommendation would you make?

💬 **Suppose revenue were** constant. I would improve profitability by reducing costs.

💬 **Suppose it were** a startup development case. Would you focus on developing customers first or building a product nobody wants to buy?

⇒ Interjections and Exclamations

there we go!	here we go!	there they go!	there you go!	I love it
fantastic	for god sake	my gosh	awesome	phenomenal
bravo	come on	bingo	absolutely	brilliant
excellent	incredible	hang it!	fabulous	marvelous
baloney	wonderful	nothing to say	alright	enjoy
great	good heavens	heavens	hey	alas
really	indeed	perfect	what	my goodness
nah	no problem	no way	nope	nuts
super	swell	welcome	well	help
please	poof	I am␣spechless	totally different	bing bang boom

- 💬 Here we go!
- 💬 There we go!
- 💬 There you go!
- 💬 Great! **I love it!**
- 💬 **Enjoy!** Have fun!
- 💬 **Bingo!** I found it!
- 💬 **Super!** That's great!
- 💬 **Huh!** I have no idea.
- 💬 **Nah!** It'll never work.
- 💬 **Man!** Forget about it!
- 💬 **No problem.** It's Ok.
- 💬 **Help!** Anybody here?
- 💬 **Really!** Are you sure?
- 💬 **Swell!** How intelligent!
- 💬 **No way!** Are you kidding?
- 💬 **Mama mia!** You're terrific!
- 💬 **Heavens!** Are you serious?
- 💬 **Ha-ha!** That was really fun!
- 💬 And **poof!** He disappeared.
- 💬 **Great!** I'm glad to hear that.
- 💬 Just **perfect!** Nothing to say!
- 💬 **Aww!** That's so kind of you!

TALK

- 💬 Oh, **hang it!** It slipped away.
- 💬 **Nuts!** I wish it were Monday.
- 💬 **Alas**, it was too good to be true.
- 💬 **Fantastic!** I couldn't do it better!
- 💬 **Come on!** You can't be serious.
- 💬 **My goodness!** What a great news!
- 💬 **Nope!** I don't know how to do it.
- 💬 **Hey!** Over here! Don't you see me?
- 💬 **Well**, so what do you recommend?
- 💬 **My goodness!** What a terrible news!
- 💬 **OK**, sounds pretty good. Let's do that.
- 💬 **Marvelous!** This design is just perfect.
- 💬 **Bravo!** Congratulations! Nicely done!
- 💬 The prototype is ready. Oh, **excellent!**
- 💬 Oh, **baloney!** How come that possible?
- 💬 **Indeed!** It could become a global crisis.
- 💬 **Fabulous!** It was a great vacation retreat!
- 💬 **Brilliant!** This idea is absolutely brilliant.
- 💬 You finished two days earlier? **Awesome!**
- 💬 **Wow!** That was an excellent presentation!
- 💬 **Hmm.** Give me some time to think it over.
- 💬 **Good heavens!** Why did that happen again?

TALK

- 💬 **Aw**, a diner of schmucks! That's messed-up!
- 💬 **What?** The World Trade Center in flames?
- 💬 **For God's sake**, take this picture out of my office!
- 💬 Can I have a coffee, **please**? Make it short, thanks!
- 💬 And **bing bang boom**! We tripled sales in no time.
- 💬 **Welcome.** Please, come in! Make yourself at home!
- 💬 **Cheers**, team! Raise a toast for this exceptional contract!
- 💬 **Jeez!** I don't know what you're talking about. What's the problem?
- 💬 **There they go!** Any time I talk about motivation, someone asks a pay raise.
- 💬 **My gosh!** In this factory, they have got restaurants, movie theaters, gyms, swimming pools, and even hospitals. (3)

⇒ On Emotions

embarrassing	shocking	quite a shock	sense of pride	hard feelings
lose temper	it's a shame	shameful	get angry at	feel sad
laughter/ smile	wounded pride	matter of pride	be proud	a bit of a shock
be happy/ happiness	mood/ state of mind	make someone angry	leave a bit to be desired	doubt/ be doubtful
be boring to death	be dull/ be uninteresting	be unhappy	be freaking out	be shocked

TALK

be upset	be annoyed at	feel offended	be nervous	be hard on someone
be out of temper	be angry at	be mad at	anxious/ anxiety	stressed/ stress

- Long meetings are invariably **dull** and **boring**.
- It's not about money. It's just **a matter of pride**.
- The client is **out of temper** as a result of the delay.
- The hostage was **shocked** at the end of the gunshot.
- He was a good guy and always had **a smile** on his face.
- I wanted to keep it professional, but he was **freaking out**.
- He's going to start **freaking out** if you don't solve it quickly.
- This client may become very irritable and easily **lose his temper**.
- Creativity is a source of **personal fulfillment, pride**, and job satisfaction.
- You should never **feel nervous** when making a recommendation to a client.
- It is **quite a shock** to learn that, at 51, your husband has Alzheimer's disease.
- **I am angry at** the government for the position they have taken in the conflict.
- Your remarks on pay cuts have caused **a bit of a shock** and a stir among employees.
- **I am really upset** that you interfered in a court case without even seeking my approval.

TALK

- The president came out with **a large smile** on his face to say the problem will be solved quickly.

- There has never been any **dull or uninteresting moment** in my long conversation with Elon.

- Sometimes staffs are not on the ball (working) as they should be, and the manager **gets quite annoyed**.

- **It's a shame** that the diagrams are so poor-looking, and the overall readability **leaves a bit to be desired**.

- There are no **hard feelings** about Steve Jobs leaving Apple, and the company is still very optimistic about the future.

- The community has a right to **feel offended** by the racist behaviors, and the government should firmly grapple with all this.

- You've **been too hard** on your staff. With their **wounded pride**, they will ask themselves why they should be loyal to you.

- **Laughter** is the best medicine as it builds muscle strength, burns calories, reduces **anxiety**, and improves overall **mood**.

Expressions for Small Talks

- accept a challenge
- acquaintance/ relationships
- all rolled up into
- alleviate pain
- appeal to customers
- appeal to emotions
- appeal to senses
- at the end of the day
- avoid trouble
- back to the drawing board
- basically/ roughly
- be a far cry from
- be imprinted of
- be in the footsteps of
- be in trouble
- be keen/ wish
- be politically correct
- bear the burden of
- bend over backward
- breathe a sigh of relief
- breathe a word
- build relationships
- business acquaintance
- by trade/ by training
- carry your burden
- catch on the way in
- cause a lot of trouble
- close collaboration
- close relationships
- come to terms with
- commuter rush hours (9:30-16)
- cope with/ deal with
- critical attitude
- cry tears of happiness
- defiant attitude
- destroy relationships
- did you ever ask yourself if …?
- DNA
- drop somth. or somn. off
- during my spare time
- during my time at
- excite curiosity
- face a challenge
- fall for something
- feel ashamed
- feel comfortable
- feel confident
- feel dizzy
- feel like something
- feel sick

TALK

- feel sorry for somebody
- first draft
- firsthand/ yourself
- from my end/ as for me
- get a head start/ start early
- get a move on/ start early
- get along with somebody
- get down to business
- get into the meat
- get to grips with/ deal with
- get to know each other
- give a hand/ help
- give your opinion
- give your take
- grant authorization
- have a discussion with
- have a minute
- have a moment
- have a snack
- have a talk with
- have a word with
- have diner
- have lunch/ have brunch
- have an impediment
- have everything tied together
- have in depth conversations
- have the time of your life
- have your heart set on
- having second thoughts
- here's the deal
- hostile attitude
- I am open to criticism
- I am open to suggestions
- I can do without it
- I can't help/ I can't resist
- I have been oblivious
- I play it safe
- in the bosom of/ in unison
- inner circle
- it doesn't make any sense
- it is going to be another story
- it makes sense
- it resonates with me
- it sounds good
- it's believed to be
- it's no surprise that
- it's purported to be
- it's understood to be
- it's not a certainty
- it's not worth the trouble
- let's jump in/ let's begin
- let's jump right in
- lighten burdens
- long haul/ long term
- long story short

TALK

make a difference	make a stop off	make a very good point	make acquaintance/ meet	make do with
menacing attitude	most commonly traveled road	most of all	move forward	my favorite [..] is
occur/ happen	crop up/ pop up	off-peak hours (6-9:30; 6-19)	on the ball/ working	on the line/ at-risk
one at a time/ one by one	one can argue that	one can assume that	one can expect that	one can notice that
one can say that	one can see that	one can wonder why	per se/ in and on itself	personal acquaintance
play down/ minimize	play it by ear	play it safe	prevent from doing something	purported to be
raise curiosity	remember hardly	remember rightly	remember vaguely	safe commute
safe travels	satisfy curiosity	save a lot of trouble	shake a leg/ speed up	shake hands
share your point of view	share your view	shoot the shit/ trivial chat	small talks/ chit chat	something just came up
something went wrong	spoil somebody's appetite	stand your ground	start over again	step up/ accelerate
steppingstone	stick to your decision	stop by/ make a stop off	suffer greatly	suffer severely

TALK

sustain relationships	take a risk/take a chance	talk ambitiously	talk openly	talk passionately
tell fibs/ lie	the irony is that	this is not self-evident	underway/ happening	unsettling/ disconcerting
warm up/ get warmed up	we have left that open	we have not won the day yet	what's going on?	what's the deal?

- What's going on? You look so sad!
- I wish you safe travels. See you soon.
- Forget about it. It's not worth the trouble.
- I heard you very well. Now, what's the deal?
- Something went wrong. The web site is down.
- Just drop it off on my desk, I'll look at it later.
- Natural gas costs roughly the same as gasoline.
- This movie raised my curiosity about Silicon Valley.
- Did you have a safe commute with this crazy traffic?
- I trust your judgment, but I'd like to try it firsthand.
- Sounds good to me. So, I'll see you on Monday at ten.
- It's no surprise that those who play it too safe earn less.
- The manager and Steve are actually close relationships.
- These new cars will save us a lot of trouble on the field.
- I never hike mountains because it makes me feel dizzy.

TALK

- Something just came up. I have to leave. I'll see you later.
- Please, feel free to share your views on the plan proposed.
- The irony in writing is that simple papers are hard to write.
- During my spare time, I do treadmill workouts to stay healthy.
- Do you have a second, please? I want to show you something.
- Many people love reading, but they never have a minute for it.
- I always encourage children to talk openly about their feelings.
- I share your views on the importance of sleeping very strongly.
- One can see that this salad is a far cry from a homemade meal.
- Take a chance at this new position. You might find it rewarding.
- People need time to come to terms with the leadership change.
- One can argue that aliens exist, but there is no evidence of that.
- We have made notable progress, but we've not won the day yet.
- Please, give me a minute to warm up before we get into the meat.
- With all the obvious problems, one can wonder why they signed.
- What's the matter with you? Why are you aggressive with people?
- Here's the deal. Bootstrapping is scalable while freelancing is not.
- It's difficult, but we have to make do with none of these resources.
- You better get a move on because the postal office will close soon.
- If you have a moment, please give us a hand with our new research.
- Making cheap and efficient cars is the DNA of Japanese carmakers.
- People are too smart and well informed to fall for a mere sales pitch.

TALK

- I look at that as a real challenge that can **cause a lot of trouble** as well.

- To succeed in this firm, you must **build and sustain good relationships**.

- I want something that works for a **long haul**, not just a week or a month.

- Let's **get a move on**! We only have until October 25 to show the work!

- I remember only **vaguely** from my business school days, long, long ago.

- Most of all, trust yourself to develop the skills that will **make a difference**.

- We **bend over backward** when an official from headquarters visits our office.

- Many Uber cabs are not running at capacity during the **commuter rush hours**.

- My advice is to focus on **making a difference**, not on being politically correct.

- This amusing statement makes **very good points** about people. Don't you agree?

- Migrating to another country can be a difficult and quite **unsettling** experience.

- **From my perspective**, I see no reason why we would want to delay the installation.

- **Long story short**. The point is the prototype is not meeting requirements.

- Work out a plan to apply the new rules **one at a time**, with good communication.

- It's been an honor to work with brilliant people **during my time** as a consultant at ABC.

- With some clients, it's better **to shoot the shit** for a while before **getting down to business.**

- **From a** cost-benefit **perspective, it doesn't make sense** to apply the full set of requirements.

- Of course, moving to cloud computing is a good solution, but **it's going to be another story.**

- You cannot do everything. My best advice is to choose one career and **stick to that decision.**

- How did you set the times and locations for **off-peak hours** and **rush hours** in the software?

- **In general, one can say that** when you are watched by someone, the way you behave changes.

- It's not knowledge **per se** that is power. It's the ability to act on the knowledge that is power. (4)

- I am an engineer **by training**, and now I am the head of global recruiting at Bain & Company.

- **One can notice that** in international forums, communications **are imprinted of** extreme courtesy.

- Sadly, all children can't grow up **in the bosom of** the family. Instead, many live in children's homes.

- For me, the plaintiff **bears the burden** of proof in establishing that he or she has been arbitrarily rated.

- The survey doesn't target Customs administration **per se**, but the overall perceptions of corruption.

- He never plans things properly ahead of time. He **plays it by ear** once situations **pop up**. That's a problem.

- **One can expect,** however, **that** the cost of outsourcing will be lower than that of hiring a full-time worker.

- **One can assume that** Chloroquine is an effective treatment against COVID-19, but it is still to be proven.

- Being realistic is the **most commonly traveled road** to poor performance. Let's be crazy sometimes.

- Senior management people tend to avoid any kind of risky projects and prefer **to play it safe** with proven ideas.

- The rising death toll of COVID-19 is forcing us to **have second thoughts** on the necessity to confine people.

- In an interview for CNN, the republican representative **gave his take** on the sustainability of the economic stimulus.

- Being an independent consultant means you're the bookkeeper, the marketer, the secretary, **all rolled up into one.**

- Some ambitious entrepreneurs are **walking in the footsteps** of Peter Thiel, resolutely aiming at building monopolies.

- Until I had finally got the project **underway,** I didn't **breathe a word** about it to anyone, not even to my closest friends.

- Mr. McMillan, I wanted to **drop this off** personally and **make your acquittance.** I thought I'd catch you **on the way in.**

- If **you stand your ground** in a negotiation, you will find that the final offer is not so final, and the deadline is not as rigid as it is **purported to be.**

- Medical decisions **are understood to be** limited to objective and verified medical facts. That's why chloroquine is not a proven treatment yet.

- Currently, the company allocates 200 dollars per year for each staff towards training, **a far cry from** the 1,000 dollars provided annually in previous years.

- If you **have your heart set on** forming a disruptive company, then you might be having the wrong momentum. Because incremental improvements work better than disruption.

Speak Like an Executive

⇒ Make Cautious Statements

No Caution	⟺	Caution
Always	⟺	Everything else being equal
Always	⟺	If and only if
Always	⟺	Most of the time
Always	⟺	Provided certain criteria
Always	⟺	Provided that
Always	⟺	Under most circumstances
Approval	⟺	Conditional approval
Certain	⟺	Subject to respect for
Certain	⟺	To be treated with caution
Certainly	⟺	Assuming everything goes perfectly
It is	⟺	It is alleged to be
It is	⟺	It is allegedly
It is	⟺	It is presumably
It is	⟺	It is reportedly
It is	⟺	It is supposedly
It is	⟺	It's yet to be confirmed that
It will realize	⟺	Assuming everything goes perfectly

It will realize	⟺	I have to warrant caution due to uncertainty
It will realize	⟺	It's subject to certain conditions
It will realize	⟺	It's subject to the condition that
It's settled	⟺	It's subject to approval
Mandatory	⟺	Advised
Mandatory	⟺	Recommended
Mandatory	⟺	Strongly recommended
Necessary	⟺	Advised
Necessary	⟺	Recommended
Necessary	⟺	Strongly recommended
We affirm	⟺	Considered with caution
We affirm	⟺	On a prudent and informed basis
We inform	⟺	As the thinking goes
We inform	⟺	The word goes that
We think	⟺	We suspect
Yes or no	⟺	On condition that the rules are complied with
Yes or no	⟺	With the available information

TALK

⇒ Speak with Authority

firmly resists	act firmly	respond firmly	deal firmly with
do firmly	forcefully act	act strongly	forceful action
act resolutely	tackle resolutely	pursue forcefully	have a firm stance
act with firmness	firmly and resolutely	fulfil your role resolutely	vigorously intervene
vigorously call for elimination	prosecuted with full vigour	act promptly and decisively	decisively grapple with
defend your views with firmness	with firmness and confidence	decide with firmness and confidence	strongly and consistently comply with

💬 We shall keep in this direction **firmly and resolutely**.

💬 We will **act decisively** to adopt an anti-harassment policy.

💬 It means defending our stakes **with firmness** but without violence.

TALK

- Gender-based violence will be recognized and **persecuted with full vigor**.

- Every attempt to dissipate the facts from people's minds will **be firmly resisted**.

- We **acted decisively** to make our offices a non-discriminatory workplace.

- In most cases, rulings should be given with the appropriate **firmness and confidence**.

- The Commission **must vigorously intervene** to obtain a swift solution to this situation.

- The firm is set to **act quickly and decisively** to the fast-changing business environment.

- It must **be done firmly** and pressed to its legitimate strength, but it must be done fairly.

- I **repeated our position firmly** and again demanded the withdrawal of this paragraph.

- The company will **act with firmness** and bring into force the individual measures envisaged.

- We are pursuing a clear policy and will take a **firm stance** on the issues discussed in the media.

- We **have vigorously called** for the total elimination of dangerous products in our factories.

- For the time being, our company is fulfilling its role properly, **resolutely defending** commercial stakes.

- The situation will only get worse if the CEO doesn't **intervene promptly and firmly** to downsize the company.

- The Crisis Committee reacted swiftly-within hours of the oil spills and **with determination** to limit the damages.
- We also request the **forceful action** of the government to put an end to ongoing unfair international trade practices.
- Today, we must **act resolutely** to significantly reduce the carbon footprint of our firm in the foreseeable future.
- The international community must **respond firmly** to the attacks of the rebels, to safeguard its people and its premises.
- Such reforms need to be **pursued forcefully** together with improvements in food processing, catering, and distribution.
- For the time being, we are **decisively grappling with** the challenges brought on by the merger, such as the integration of new business units into the reporting chain.

Talk to Your Team

⇒ On Motivation

- ❞ I will not **ask you to do anything** I will not do myself. (5)
- ❞ I will not **ask you to go anywhere** I will not go myself. (5)
- ❞ This **problem** is nowhere close to the end of the world.
- ❞ Every new team is, to some extent, **ineffective at the start**.
- ❞ We lost the battle this time around, but we'll **rebound** quickly.
- ❞ You have delivered **over and beyond expectations** in this project.
- ❞ You are leaving a strong **footprint** in this company for a long time ahead.
- ❞ It's the ability to act on **knowledge** that is power. Not the knowledge in itself.
- ❞ We are one team, one mission, one responsibility. I will **never let you down**.

TALK

- 💬 **At the end of the day**, we are going to kick the ass of coronavirus out of the State. (5)

- 💬 I want you to be happy to **give** the highest version of **yourself** in this project. Have fun!

- 💬 I am **delighted to join** this team because what you are doing here means a lot to so many people.

- 💬 **I am proud** but humble to lead a team that is way more skilled and experienced than myself.

- 💬 Every hour you spend on the ball *(working)* contributes to **making** the **life** of a family someway **better**.

- 💬 **What you are doing** every single day from your desk **matters** to thousands of clients who rely on you.

- 💬 **I am so proud** and admirative of the work you have been doing amidst the crisis to keep the project underway.

- 💬 **Being realistic** is the most commonly traveled road to poor performance. Let's be crazy sometimes.

- 💬 I just want to let you know that I am satisfied with the **hard work** you're doing with low resources but high expectations.

- 💬 We must be open about the challenges we're facing and how we're working to address them as a way to **lead with transparency**.

- 💬 **I am impressed** by the **quality of this team**, to the extent that I am feeling like an intern. That is to say that I am joining you as a **humble** person rather than a maven.

- 💬 This **challenge** is tough, but we can decide to make it one of the most creative endeavors of our carriers. That's why **I give you leeway** for all decisions in your respective units.

- 💬 I know some of you are **working around the clock** to contain this issue. I want to let you know that what you are doing is vital, and you will be rewarded for all your time and effort.

⇒ On Communication

- 💬 Do you think it **makes sense**?
- 💬 I trust your **judgment**; let's do this.
- 💬 What do you think? Does it **make sense**?
- 💬 To be honest, I don't think it's a **good idea**.
- 💬 Sounds good. Can you **tell me more about** it?
- 💬 That's precisely **the point** I was trying to make.
- 💬 **Any update** on the health project engagement?
- 💬 The **credit goes to** Alicia for taking the initiative.
- 💬 Any **feedback** on the proposal will be appreciated.
- 💬 **Where do we stand** on the health project engagement?
- 💬 There is a **communication problem** that cuts across all this.
- 💬 We don't **operate** on opinions; we **operate** on data and facts. (5)
- 💬 Our **customers** don't buy what we do. They buy why we do it. (6)
- 💬 **Special attention** must be paid to the definition of requirements.
- 💬 We are going to leverage the founder's **story** and the customers' stories.
- 💬 This **resolution** must be applied across the board with immediate effect.

- It's much better to keep slides simple with no more than three points per **slide**.
- **Innovation** comes from adversity, so it's time to rethink the way we do business.
- **Stories** always work because they make clients connect with the brand and build loyalty.
- I would like to ask each of you, one by one, to **weigh in** on the decision we have to make.
- In most cases, it's good to have **competition**, but not so aggressive as to be a threat to the company.
- Often, we become impatient because **progress** is not as discernable and immediate as we want. (7)
- As usual, make sure you add at least one three-word format of **value proposition** among the suggestions.
- **Our goal is** not to hire a marketer who needs a job. We need to hire a marketer who believes in what we believe. (6)
- We recommend that you reinforce your **brand**'s vision and keep customers at the heart of your communications.
- I want to **introduce** a new staff, Mr. Jerry Wright. He's been transferred from the Shanghai Office. Dear Jerry, **welcome on board**. Do you want to say something?

⇒ On Effectiveness and efficiency

- Please, **keep it short**. Less is more.
- We need to **focus** on the most urgent matters.

- 💬 Let's not lose sight of what actually is **our priority**.
- 💬 We need to have something **up and running** by July.
- 💬 **Who's responsible** for the organization of the workshop?
- 💬 Rigorous **accountability** must be applied across the board.
- 💬 You must **fit in** quickly if you want to succeed in this firm.
- 💬 Unfortunately, it won't **make any difference** if you just cut prices.
- 💬 **Our goal** is not to disrupt but to make incremental improvement.
- 💬 **Our goal** is to generate cash flows in the future. All else are tactics.
- 💬 Let's **lay one brick at a time**. We can't do all this at the same time.
- 💬 This story **makes very good points** about the buying decision-making.
- 💬 We are **running late on the agenda**. Do you have any suggestions to **cut corners**?
- 💬 This **urgency** implies that all staff must focus **all their efforts on** this end until it is achieved.
- 💬 The best things are worth the wait. The new **deadline** of the supplier is put off to next week.
- 💬 If we **choose wisely**, we will save ourselves a considerable amount of work versus trying to do everything. (3)
- 💬 As a young graduate with little experience, I don't pretend to know what is right. But **I would suggest** that we make the project lean and flexible, then we can iterate with adjustable short-term plans.

Speak Like a Consultant

- **The helicopter view/ the big picture**

   All these expressions refer to the situation as a whole or the big picture.

   Example: As we have covered all the details, it will be more efficient now to look at <u>the big picture</u>.

- **80/20 rule**

   It is also called the Pareto Principle. It implies that 80% of the results are produced by 20% of causes.

   Example: As the 80/20 rule commands, you must focus on retaining the 20% most valuable customers as they will account for 80% of your sales.

- **Actionable**

   An adjective used to qualify a recommendation that can be acted upon or implemented.

   Example: This model is not <u>actionable</u> because we do not have the necessary data on customers' perception of brand value.

- **Add value**

   Generally, it means being productive or providing more satisfaction to customers.

   Example: We consider waste as any cost that is not <u>adding value</u> to our customers.

- **At least we now have a better idea of the questions**

   A euphemism meaning that the analysis is wrong and not even directionally correct.

Example: We are back to the drawing board. At least we now have a better idea of the questions.

At the end of the day

This expression refers to the outcome of a task or activity. This point usually concerns the ultimate results or deliverables.

Example: This is a simple engagement, so I will not supervise every step. However, <u>at the end of the day,</u> I want to receive positive feedback from the client.

Back to the drawing board

An expression meaning, we return to the beginning of an analysis or a process to restart, because it isn't working.

Example: If the board produces a "no" vote, realistically, the acquisition will be dead, and we'll be <u>back to the drawing board</u>.

Bandwidth

This word means the availability of time or resources.

Example: I want an experienced associate for this project. Does Jerry have enough <u>bandwidth</u> at this moment?

Beach/bench

The status of the Consultant with no engagement.

Example: In this firm, when you are <u>on the beach</u> for more than two weeks, you must do something, or soon you'll be searching for a new job.

Best of breed

A superior thing among various alternatives.

◆ *Example: SAP leverages* best-of-breed *ERP technology to offer a solution that allows companies to integrate business functions seamlessly.*

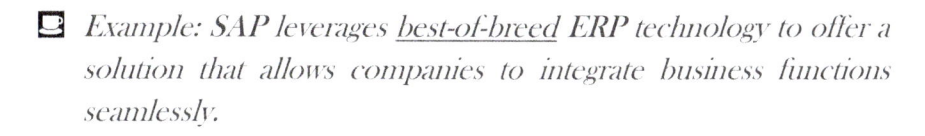

♞ Best practices

Common practices or methods which are considered to produce better results as compared with alternatives.

◆ *Example: When working in teams, we can share* best practices *and processes to be more efficient.*

♞ Black Swan

An unpredictable event with considerable effects, developed by the famous statistician Nassim Taleb.

◆ *Example: The current crisis is a* black swan *because it's an extreme event with very high costs but very low probability of occurring.*

♞ Blanks

PowerPoint slides outlined in a notebook and usually turned to a business analyst or junior consultant to undertake a job.

◆ *Example: Let me make a few* blanks *to get the point across.*

♞ Boil the ocean

This expression refers to the work of the consultant who is lacking focus. It means doing much more than needed to come to a figure or result.

◆ *Example: Again, let's not try to* boil the ocean *but just identify the most essential variables.*

♞ Bottom-up

Starting from bottom elements and moving way up to reach an estimate.

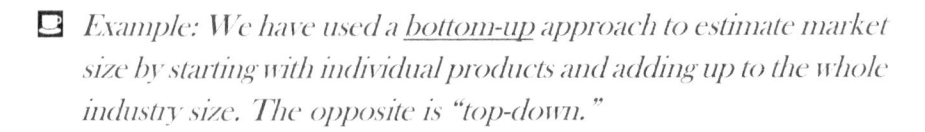

> *Example: We have used a <u>bottom-up</u> approach to estimate market size by starting with individual products and adding up to the whole industry size. The opposite is "top-down."*

♞ Buckets

Means "categories" or "groups" when structuring issues with frameworks.

> *Example: An acquisition analysis framework is usually made of three <u>buckets,</u> including the target's standalone value, synergies, and the capacity to execute the acquisition.*

♞ Buttoned-down

It qualifies a work that is done comprehensively and efficiently.

> *Example: Please get the contract <u>buttoned-down,</u> and then we'll move on to the other projects in the pipeline.*

♞ Buy-in

Informal agreement or consent.

Example: Meetings are more effective when there is an advance <u>buy-in</u> on the agenda and documents.

♞ C-suite

C-level executives (e.g., CEO, COO, CFO, CIO, CMO)

♞ Case

A consulting project, engagement, assignment, or study.

♞ Charge code

A budget code for a project to which trip and work expenses are charged.

🔹 *Example: Kindly use the following <u>charge code</u> for all expenses related the workshop: MK-P536578-00-TG0578.*

🔺 Circle back

To tackle something that was postponed for later.

🔹 *Example: I think they will <u>circle back</u> to propose an agreement and fill in the details over the next few months.*

🔺 Close the loop

A consulting jargon that means closing a resolved situation that was extensively discussed.

🔹 *Example: "Performance management and oversight practices are those which <u>close the loop</u> on accountability, authority, and responsibility." (8)*

🔺 Core client

An important client with a long-lasting relationship with a consulting firm.

🔹 *Example: we are constantly working to strengthen relationships with our <u>core client</u> base.*

🔺 Core competency

It is a strength that lies at the core of an organization and constitutes a competitive edge.

🔹 *Example: Control engineering is one of our <u>core competences</u> and is a crucial performance factor for our clients.*

🔺 Critical path

The key tasks of a process that leads to an expected result.

> *Example: Delay in <u>critical path</u> activities will invariably delay the entire project if other steps are not compressed.*

♘ Cut-Throat

Aggressive and stiff competition.

Example: Competition in the low-end automotive segment is <u>cut-throat</u>.

♘ Deck

A slide or PowerPoint presentation.

♘ Deliverable

Expected outcomes of work, project, or engagement.

> *Example: The object of this conference call is to know whether the project <u>deliverables</u> were achieved on time and within budget.*

♘ Delta

A reference to the delta in math, and simply means "change." Sometimes the word "change" is deemed frightening, so it is replaced by delta.

> *Example: The pandemic is going to affect our business. What do you think the <u>delta</u> will be?*

♘ Directionally correct

Expression meaning that there is a couple of inaccurate numbers even though the general analysis has legs.

> *Example: Roughly speaking, the analysis is <u>directionally correct</u>. Just make sure you correct and double-check the numbers.*

♘ Drill-down

An action meaning to go into the details or granularity.

> *Example: <u>Drill down</u> analysis allows the consultant to zoom from the highest to the lowest granularity of a framework.*

♞ Due dil

Abbreviation of *due diligence*. It refers to the work involved in comprehensive research or study.

> *Example: With the new regulation on the corporate takeover, more "<u>due dil</u>" will be required on acquisition targets in the US market.*

♞ The elephant in the room

The obvious problem that nobody wants to address.

> *Example: I want to return to the issue that is perhaps the most problematic and is <u>the elephant in the room</u>: is there any budget for this activity?*

♞ Elevator pitch

A brief but encompassing speech or presentation that is performed during a networking event or fund raising series.

> *Example: Startups promoters from the agriculture and data management sectors were invited to share their innovations during extremely short <u>elevator-pitches</u>.*

♞ Engagement

A consulting assignment or project, also called "case" or "study".

♞ Deep dive

Brainstorming.

> *Example: Tomorrow, we'll have a <u>deep dive</u> into the soft drink case after lunch.*

♞ Facetime

It refers to the amount of time during which one is seen in the office, making the consultant look productive.

- *Example: I don't want to be on the beach, so I go to the office on Saturday to add some facetime.*

Gain traction

To have an influential person buy in an idea. It means having a person with authority engaged in an idea or a project.

- *Example: the reform failed to gain traction at the political level.*

Greenfield

It's a new market entry opportunity corresponding to setting up a new subsidiary in the new market.

- *Example: A greenfield entry is too risky but acquiring a local company would save time and risk.*

Guesstimate

An approximate but rational calculation of the size or amount a measurement when no facts are available.

- *Example: For the items that we don't have a single guesstimate of monetary value, a separate physical accounting will be required.*

Have legs

Meaning that something sounds good.

- *Example: The internet of things trend will continue to have legs for many years ahead.*

Hit the ground running

Used when speaking about a new consultant, to describe his capacity to add value immediately on projects.

TALK

♞ *Example: The best candidates were those who possessed the skills to hit the ground running. They showed some promise of being able to reach a high level of productivity within a reasonable time.*

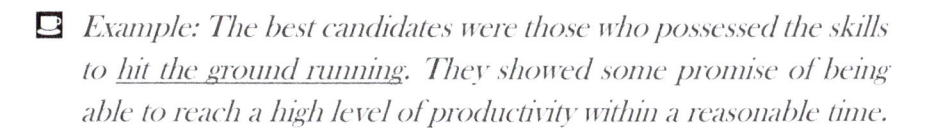

♞ **In Production Mode (IPM)**

Expression meaning that work is in progress and not completed yet.

♞ *Example: The market sizing is IPM, but not for a long time.*

♞ **Leverage**

It's frequently used in consulting and means putting a resource at work to generate expected results.

♞ *Example: For the upcoming fiscal year, our performance will depend on our capacity to leverage our core capabilities to innovate.*

♞ **Low-hanging fruit**

It refers to something that can be completed quickly or easily.

♞ *Example: For the first upcoming year, the startup should aim at low-hanging fruits in underserved market segments.*

♞ **Managing up**

Providing feedback to help superiors perform their job better. It also includes keeping these superiors in the loop, while anticipating and solving issues for them. This skill is a real value-add for junior consultants. (9)

♞ **MECE**

Mutually Exclusive, Collectively Exhaustive. An important standard for undertaking cases, making hypotheses, or building models.

♞ **Mission-critical**

Used to qualify a resource or work that cannot be replaced by something else. It can be a product, an analysis, or a service that is crucial.

> *Example: We are applying the Lean Startup model in this venture. So, all expenses that are not <u>mission-critical</u> must be cut out.*

Move the needle

Get your team to make a great additional effort to achieve the desired outcome.

> *Example: Cold calls are not giving satisfactory results hitherto; we need to <u>move the needle</u> with direct mailing.*

On the line

Is used to describe something at stake or in danger.

> *Example: Hundreds of jobs are <u>on the line</u> as a result of ongoing restructuring.*

On the same page

It means to share the same view about something.

> *Example: Let's read the minutes once more to make sure we're <u>on the same page</u>.*

Organic growth

As opposed to mergers and acquisitions, it represents the increase in production level and customer base without acquiring any other business entity.

> *Example: The company is aggressively pursuing its <u>organic growth</u> strategy as they are too small to acquire other firms.*

Peeling the onion

TALK

Expression meaning that the consultants are still figuring out what the client wants.

📧 *Example: We are on the right track, but we need to <u>peel some more onion</u> to get to the crux of the matter.*

🔸 **Pipe or pipeline**

Potential upcoming projects for a consulting firm. It includes projects in the sales cycle of the firm.

📧 *Example: We have lost another client! I want to have a meeting with you tomorrow. We are going to review all the projects in the <u>pipe</u>.*

🔸 **Progress review**

A regular meeting to monitor results and performance periodically. It may also refer to a professional performance review for an engagement.

🔸 **Push back**

It refers to the fact of reporting difficulty or challenge preventing the consultant from performing his job. It usually happens when there is an overpromise, unrealistic expectation, or a burnout of the consultant. (9)

🔸 **Raise the bar**

An expression meaning to set standards or expectations at a higher level.

📧 *Example: The end of the monopoly of AT&T in 1984 <u>has raised the bar</u> in the US telecommunication market.*

🔸 **Rock star**

A term that refers to great performer with remarkable competencies, outstanding results, and is often in high demand for new projects.

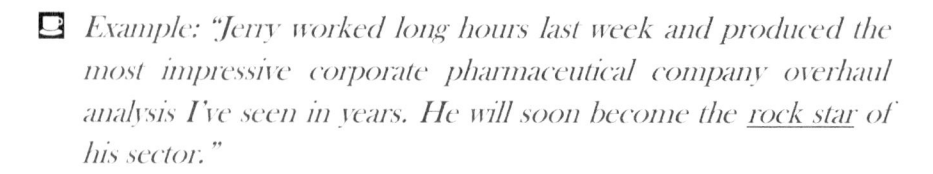

◨ *Example: "Jerry worked long hours last week and produced the most impressive corporate pharmaceutical company overhaul analysis I've seen in years. He will soon become the <u>rock star</u> of his sector."*

♞ Safe bet

Something that is not risky, also known as a "home run."

◨ *Example: It's a <u>safe bet</u> that most people will not change with time.*

♞ Scaling

It means expanding the business to serve a wider market through organic growth or mergers and acquisitions.

◨ *Example: If you are serious about launching a startup, you must go after small markets first. If those markets are able to expand, you can <u>scale into</u> a large business that is highly differentiated and hard to compete with.*

♞ Seachange

A substantial change in the business model of the company.

◨ *Example: The new way retail banks interact with their clients in the past decade in terms of how they prioritize customers is a true <u>seachange</u>.*

♞ See something through

Proceed with a job until it is fully completed.

◨ *Example: If we don't <u>see</u> the engagement <u>through</u> by July, we will dismiss the consultant.*

♞ Smell test

It is the intuition about the soundness of a given result using common sense and experience.

> *Example: This result fails to pass the <u>smell test</u>, simply because it means the market size is lower than the market share of the leader.*

Smooth sailing

When success is achieved without a hitch (without problems).

> *Example: A new CEO has been appointed. Ever since it's been <u>smooth sailing</u>.*

Straw man

It's the outline of a document without the full content.

Study

A consulting project, engagement, assignment, or case.

The right road, but the wrong direction

An expression meaning that the engagement team will be recomposed because the analysis was poorly done.

> *Example: For the Bionade case, I think we found the right road, but we took the wrong direction.*

Think out of the box

It means being original or creative when solving a problem or dealing with an issue by providing a very new way of solving them.

Tighten up/clean up

It means making the final arrangements and corrections of your deliverables—think spell check, grammar, style, etc.

Tipping point

It's the critical point at which a series of small changes becomes substantial to cause larger, more significant effects.

Touch base

Expression meaning to catch up with a person with whom you've not had much contact lately.

> *Example: "I've been dealing with another client all week, and I know I owe you some numbers. We'll <u>touch base</u> after my afternoon conference call." (9)*

♞ Top-down

It refers to developing an estimate by starting with the highest-level assumptions and deriving lower level estimates by drilling down progressively.

> *Example: We recommend a <u>top-down</u> approach so that the corporate budget will be developed by starting with global allocations made at the strategic level and tickle down to business and operational levels.*

♞ Up or out

It's an internal promotion policy, which means if you're not promoted, you're laid off. Not all firms use this policy formally or informally, but many do. It's always good to know.

♞ Uphill battle

It is a difficult job that implies obstacles and challenges.

> *Example: This acquisition is going to be an <u>uphill battle</u> because the senior management defeated several attempts in the past.*

♞ Upper hand

It's the fact of having more power and control over other people.

> *Example: With my long experience in cloud computing, I had the <u>upper hand</u> in the technical aspects.*

♞ Upward feedback

It's the practice of providing feedback to more senior employees.

🔸 Utilization rate

It's the occupation rate of the consultant. It is the client service hours performed over total available work hours. If the figure is below 50%, the consultant will be "right-sized" (10).

🔸 Value-add

A takeoff on "value-added" based on the notion of increasing shareholder wealth. Now it is used to describe anything that "adds value," i.e., is positive, productive, and helpful.

   📇 *Example: Consultants are clearly <u>value-add</u> professionals.*

🔸 Waterfall

It is a broken bar chart that displays the cumulative effect of sequentially introduced positive or negative values. If the next figure is positive, its bar grows up from the height of the former bar. If the next figure is negative, its bar falls, starting at the height of the former bar. It's been made popular by McKinsey, *Example:*

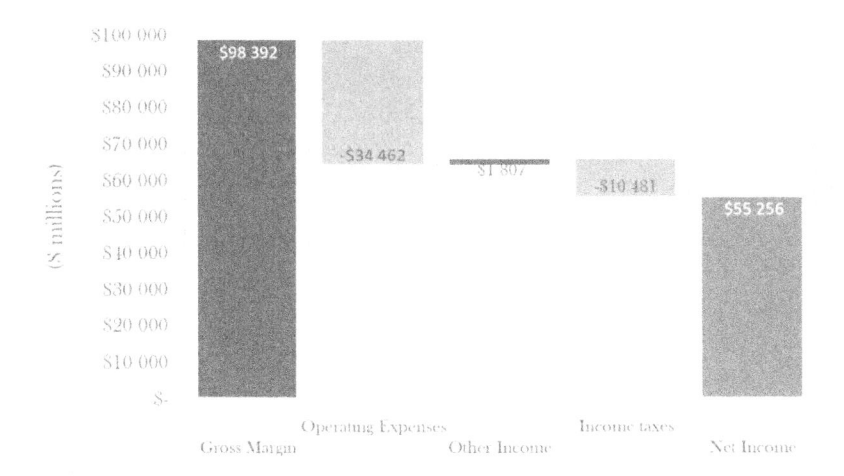

Figure 1. Net Income Waterfall of Apple Inc. for the fiscal year ended September 28, 2019

TALK

♞ **We've left that open**

An expression meaning that we didn't think about it until someone asked.

▣ *Example: How will this affect the current marketing campaign? We've left that open.*

♞ **Weeds**

The complex details of a consulting analysis, which is not useful when presenting.

▣ *Example: Please, remove all the <u>weed</u> from the slides, because we don't have the time for that.*

♞ **White space**

An opportunity for a firm to make sales where it is not operating yet.

▣ *Example: A high-income country where there is no McDonald restaurant is a <u>white space</u> for the company.*

♞ **Wordsmith**

Performing unnecessary edits to a text that won't significantly change the content. Usually, it's not about cutting the jargon which must be stripped when writing.

♞ **Workplan**

A schedule for starting and delivering an engagement or the different steps of the assignment's execution. It is a mission-critical issue in every consulting assignment.

Learn More Transition Words

⇒ Introduction

initially	ever since	first of all	first	firstly
here's the deal	first and foremost	in the first place	in the beginning	at the outset
at the beginning	at the first sight	to start with	back in/ a while ago	for one thing

💬 **Initially,** we had a series of meetings with line managers.

💬 **Back in** the late 90s, we were massively investing in tech startups.

💬 **First,** we need to look back and talk about the inception of the project.

💬 **First and most importantly,** we need to change the way we serve our customers.

💬 **For one thing,** I want to make it clear that I have no experience in cloud computing.

💬 **When I first started** working a year ago, I was working for a construction company in Delaware.

- 💬 **First of all,** I want to say that this activity is more of a sharing of experience than a formal training.
- 💬 **Ever since** this new CEO has taken office, we have seen a culture of secrecy develop in the company.
- 💬 **In the first place,** we need to focus on how to create a good business model before covering the financial details.
- 💬 **First and foremost,** we recommend **that** the company leverage internal talent by promoting more insiders to senior-level positions.

⇒ Developing

next/ then/ also/ and/ too	further/ furthermore	in addition/ additionally	in the second place	in the third place
subsequently/ afterward	as far as ... is concerned	from a ... perspective	not only ... but also	similarly/ in the same way
in one form or another	in some respects	in one way or another	as a matter of fact	in the same vein
in that vein	along the way	to this end	actually	increasingly
moreover	arguably	over and above	another ... is	in fact
note that	typically	to some extent	in this respect	in other words
on top of that	that is to say	in most cases	in that case	by the way

- 💬 **Next,** we will focus on sales and marketing.
- 💬 Shortly **afterward,** we will have a VC with London.

TALK

- 💬 **Moreover**, the license appears to be very easy to secure.
- 💬 **In the same vein**, I also want to highlight these critical steps.
- 💬 **As a matter of fact**, your greatest weakness is lack of focus.
- 💬 **As far as** our department **is concerned**, no staff will be laid off.
- 💬 **Similarly**, poor customer service has led to a higher churn rate.
- 💬 **Furthermore**, it is essential to monitor competitors' prices closely.
- 💬 **Not only will** this reduce inventory, **but it will also** reduce storage costs.
- 💬 **Along the way**, we worked towards achieving gender parity at all levels.
- 💬 **From a** branding **perspective**, we'll focus on design, PR, and advertising.
- 💬 Energy means **not only** hydrocarbons **but also** electricity and renewable energies.
- 💬 **While** progress has been made **in some respects**, the project **still** has a long way to go.
- 💬 **To this end**, ABC has developed a more restrictive external communication policy.
- 💬 **In addition to that**, the development team will adopt the Scrum framework for agile meetings.
- 💬 **On top of that**, ABC has also provided free medicaments to solve the problems of delivery on the field.
- 💬 Identifying and addressing the untapped segments is **also** part of the low hanging fruits mentioned earlier.
- 💬 **Moreover**, Public administrations play an essential role in attracting both individual and institutional investors.

TALK

> The current projects address country risks **to some extent**, but there is no coordinated risk management plan.

> **In the same way**, the results of these negotiations are to be approved before the agreement becomes binding.

> **Additionally**, a capacity reinforcement in remote project management must be implemented within six months.

> **In fact**, the risk of contamination is the result of a failure to guarantee the highest quality standards throughout the food chain.

> **Over and above the** financial support, for more than five years, ABC has provided high-level technical assistance to the project.

> If you must spend time to seek promotion and **subsequently** get buried in the higher position's duties, what will this mean to your family?

⇒ Giving Examples

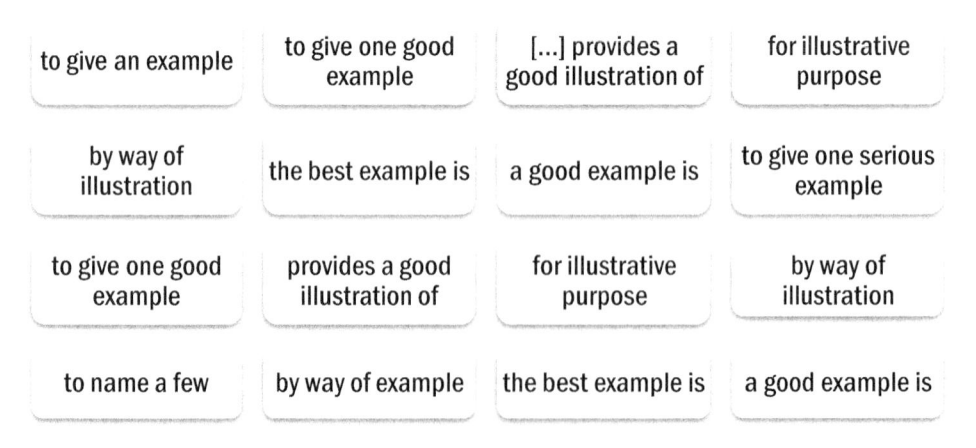

to give an example	to give one good example	[...] provides a good illustration of	for illustrative purpose
by way of illustration	the best example is	a good example is	to give one serious example
to give one good example	provides a good illustration of	for illustrative purpose	by way of illustration
to name a few	by way of example	the best example is	a good example is

> **To give an example**, Zoom allows project staff to collaborate remotely.

> **For instance**, a company can outsource non-critical tasks like packaging, delivery, and customer service.

💬 Nestle, **for instance**, has performed a couple of acquisitions lately, including Wamiz and Terrafertil, in 2018.

💬 **The best example of** high-tech products' marketing model is *Crossing the Chasm*, developed by Geoffrey Moore. (11)

💬 **For illustration purpose**, the chat application Yik Yak failed in dealing with declining market share due to resistance to change.

💬 **To illustrate that**, the blood testing technology startup Theranos failed in 2018 despite a whopping $910 million in total funding. (12)

⇒ Opposing and Comparing

on the one hand,	on the other hand,	notwithstanding	at the expense of	on the contrary
in comparison	in contrast to	all the same	nevertheless	nonetheless
in contrast	by contrast	conversely	contrary to	for all that
as though	even though	instead of	despite	in spite of
even though	instead of	despite	in spite of	but
regardless of	otherwise	alternatively	however	although
just as ... so also	whereas	while	unlike	yet

💬 **Regardless of** the outcome, we will make the full report public.

💬 **Just as** businesses compete for profit, **so also** non-profit compete for donations.

- The company made a shift toward cheap production methods **at the expense of** quality.

- **By contrast**, adapting and changing is critical in cut-throat industries like airline transportation.

- The acquisition bid had been unsuccessful, **yet** it was a positive and constructive exploration.

- **However, despite** significant progress achieved thus far, a couple of problems remain.

- It is a shame to realize that we have both the expertise and the resources, **yet** this situation still prevails.

- **Despite** the reduction in staff headcount, now we manufacture more parts per week than ever before.

- There might be more convergence and sameness in the next decade, **but** innovation will change many things **all the same**.

- Startups face an incredible amount of challenges, and there is no magic formula for success. **However**, you can improve your chances by avoiding common pitfalls.

⇒ **Setting Time**

every now and then	every once in a while	now and again	once in a blue moon	once and again
on the odd occasion	once in a great while	in the meantime	every so often	now and then
simultaneously	occasionally	sometimes	almost always	afterward

after	at last	before	currently	during
earlier	immediately	later	meanwhile	now
recently	subsequently	then	on and off	on occasion

💬 With my diet, I can eat chocolate only **occasionally**.

💬 With my new job, I can go to the gym only **once in a while**.

💬 Fortunately, such a crisis happens only **once in a blue moon**.

💬 **Meanwhile**, we got a 20% market penetration in three months.

💬 Managers have a responsibility to say 'no' **every now and then**.

💬 Such delays have happened, but they occurred only **on the odd occasion**.

💬 **Once in a great while**, a product transcends its primary function and becomes an icon.

💬 I reiterate **once and again** that defending children's right to education is critical for every society.

💬 **In the meantime**, businesses will close, and jobs will be lost as a consequence of the pandemic.

💬 **Meanwhile**, the data hitherto (so far) available are not sufficient to formulate an effective strategy to combat this problem.

💬 If you must spend time to seek promotion and **subsequently** get buried in the higher position's duties, what will this mean to your family?

TALK

⇒ Setting Scope

all the way through	day in and day out	all the way out	all the way up	all the way down
all the way to	down the road	totally/ entirely	across the board	from back to back
from cover to cover	from end to end	from start to finish	from the ground up	comprehensively
in its entirety	in all aspects	altogether	thoroughly	exhaustively
as a general rule	completely	to some extent	globally	from the inside out
from the outsite in	from the top down	from the bottom up	from the top to the bottom	from the beginning to the end

- Every new team is, **to some extent**, ineffective at the start.
- Fairtrade aims at enhancing healthy economic development **from the bottom up**.
- Unpaid leaves can vary in length from three weeks **all the way up** to two years at the maximum.
- Our engineers are working **day in and day out** to find ways to produce better energy for the planet.
- The key issues **in all aspects** of food safety legislation are the principles of traceability and transparency.
- There has been a great track record in this small-scale program because it is working **from the ground up**.
- We seize this opportunity to thank you for believing in the project and for supporting us **all the way through**.

💬 The report should examine the entire education chain from kindergarten **all the way through** to university.

💬 Every successful startup is expected to **go all the way from** idea to customer development, building, and branding.

⇒ Setting Importance

more specifically	more importantly	most importantly	it's important to note that	it should be noted
more than anything	equally important	predominantly	especially	specially
particularly	in particular	essentially	in essence	primarily
most of all	mainly	notably	mostly	above all

💬 This was **primarily** due to an increase in production costs.

💬 The division comprises **essentially** two units to produce tires and airbags.

💬 **Most of all**, trust yourself to develop the skills that will make a difference.

💬 **More specifically**, the object of the contract is the development of a new turbine.

💬 Updated business statistics are **equally important** to spur business innovation.

💬 **Equally important** is the alignment of the salary grid with a market percentile for objective compensation.

> I think that these are the basic points that need to be assessed and, **particularly**, where we need to renegotiate terms.

> **Most of all**, I'd like to inform you that this is a shady practice. We will require your written confirmation every time you do it as a way of preserving our reputation.

⇒ Setting a Condition

focusing exclusively on	while recognizing that	exclusively limited to	while accepting that
on condition that	while admitting	if and only if	supposing
provided	providing	depending on	given
exclusively	only when	only where	so long as
as long as	otherwise	only if	in case
unless	then	only	if

> The workshop will be held in two months **unless** decided **otherwise**.

> We can innovate **as long as** we question received ideas and rethink our business. (2)

> The profitability of a plant will vary **depending on** efficiencies and technical fluctuations.

> From this perspective, initial training **focusing exclusively on** technical subjects would not be suitable.

- 💬 We have come a long way in infrastructure, all the **while recognizing that** much remains to be done.
- 💬 **While admitting that** there is always a margin of error, we are reasonably confident of the results obtained.
- 💬 We will buy more **only if** the sample functions dependably under normal operating conditions and performs appropriately in exceptional situations.

⇒ Stating Causality and Consequence

as/ for/ since/ hence	that's the reason why	for the reason that	so much so that
as a consequence	this is because	on account of	consequently
as a result of	as a result	accordingly	because of
in order to	to this end	given that	so/ so that
so as to	thanks to	therefore	because

- 💬 Costs are going down mainly **as a result of** economies of scale.
- 💬 Doing advocacy for individuals can be necessary **for the reason that** they belong to a severely disadvantaged group.
- 💬 **As a consequence,** the general government debt increased rapidly from 29.4% of GDP in 2007 to 52.5% of GDP in 2011.
- 💬 **Consequently,** the pension system will remain balanced with stable contribution rates regardless of the aging of the population.

❞ Investors are increasingly wary of investing in disruptive and innovative products **because** it is not always obvious why one startup succeeds, and another one fails.

⇒ Stating Safety

safe	safely	securely	surely	unharmed
cautiously	dependably	reliably	in safety	harmlessly
in peace	certainly	peacefully	all right	risk-free
without risk	without difficulty	in complete safety	somewhere safe	alive and well
without any problem	without problems	without a hitch	without any risk	in a surefire way

❞ The engagement has been executed **without a hitch**.

❞ Let's move **cautiously** and evaluate the proposal in its entirety.

❞ No matter how wealthy we are, we all want to travel **safely and securely**.

❞ The three staff members were found **unharmed** one hour after the crash.

❞ We will buy more only if the sample functions **dependably** under all operating conditions.

❞ The virtual account would give the possibility to prospects to test their trading skills **without any risk**.

❞ In France, some of the startups are incredibly successful, and the entrepreneurial spirit **is alive and well**.

⇒ Concluding

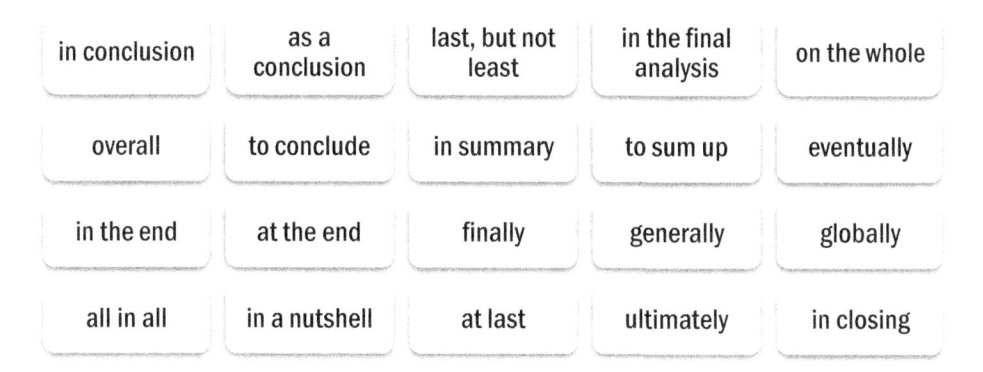

in conclusion	as a conclusion	last, but not least	in the final analysis	on the whole
overall	to conclude	in summary	to sum up	eventually
in the end	at the end	finally	generally	globally
all in all	in a nutshell	at last	ultimately	in closing

💬 **In closing**, I would like to revisit a few essential points.

💬 **To conclude**, budget overspending is essentially caused by poor financial planning.

💬 **Eventually**, investors were misled by deceitful information from the CEO of Theranos.

💬 **As a conclusion**, what suggestions can be made to improve the effects of the incentive schemes?

💬 **Last but not least**, energy means not only hydrocarbons but also electricity and renewable energy.

💬 **In conclusion**, if you are serious about launching your startup, you first need to look around for viable trends.

💬 **All in all**, the move to digital marketing, led by younger talent, is a positive step toward the refreshing of the brand.

TALK

Exercises

1. Change the words underlined.
   - We are not <u>out of danger</u> yet.
   - I want to make <u>a few</u> observations.
   - Mr. Sullivan will <u>be in charge of</u> this program.
   - We need to <u>understand</u> how the market is growing.
   - You <u>also</u> might go abroad if the economic downturn persists.
   - In this interview, Jack Ma <u>gives his opinion</u> on ending poverty.
   - This situation will <u>cause problems</u> in the security of the premises.
   - The CEO is now <u>in serious difficulty</u> after the affair was made public.
   - My field of competence <u>covers</u> system engineering and software building.
   - The crisis has caused <u>many types of</u> problems <u>concerning</u> the viability of the project.

2. Transform the following statements into cautious statements.
   - It's <u>always</u> better to start small.
   - The next iPhone <u>will be</u> transparent.
   - This company <u>is</u> close to bankruptcy.
   - The CEO <u>will</u> step down in the near future.
   - It is <u>necessary</u> to audit the sales department every year.

3. Complete the following phrases with the appropriate words.
   - I wish we _____ a coffee break before starting.
   - *(conditional expression)*
   - We need to _____ on the most urgent matters. *(talking to your team)*

- I wanted to keep it professional, but he was _____ out. *(on emotion)*
- One _____ that aliens exist, but there is no evidence of that. *(small talk)*
- It's a shame that the diagrams are so poor-looking, and the overall readability leaves a bit to be _____. *(small talk)*
- Currently, the company allocates $200 per year to each staff towards training, a far _____ from the $1,000 provided annually in previous years. *(small talk)*
- _____ analysis allows the consultant to zoom from the highest to the lowest granularity of a framework. *(speak like a consultant)*
- With all the obvious problems, one _____ why they signed. *(small talk)*
- The survey doesn't target Customs administration _____, but the overall perceptions of corruption. *(small talk)*
- There is a communication problem that _____ across all this. *(talking to your team)*

Chapter 3
IMPRESS

The ability to act on knowledge is power.
Michael Schrage

Interview for Jobs

⇒ Introduce Yourself

*****Important notice:** These personal introductions are given for entertainment purpose. The author cannot be held responsible for any unsuccessful job interview.

> ### CASE 2: IT Analyst Position Interview (Low Experience)
>
> Dear Members of the panel, I'd like first to thank you for giving me the opportunity to have this interview and eventually work for your company as an **IT Analyst**. Let me give you a quick overview of myself in five short points.
>
> My name is Jerry Knight, 26 years old. I am single and have no kid yet. I am an IT assistant by trade and training. I graduated from the University of Illinois two years ago, and my research paper covered "Database Architecture and Management in the Banking Industry." I loved technology since my childhood, and that is why I am stepping up today to become an IT Analyst.
>
> From the experience perspective, I am totaling two years that cut across IT networks, programming, and cloud computing, with a greater focus on SaaS. During those two years, I got the opportunity to work on meaningful projects where we deployed the infrastructure of a dominant online-based service provider. I developed strong analytical competencies along with some project management acumen. I learned to be an effective communicator and team player as well.
>
> About the day-to-day work, I always perform my job with high standards to deliver above expectations. At least I try. I prioritize, I set benchmarks, I collaborate, I research everything, and I always double-check my work. This is to give an overview of the analyst I am.

From my resumé, you can see my interest in topics related to IT through the certifications I completed on cybersecurity, client services, and artificial intelligence.

As a person, I am proactive, open-minded, and easy to work with. I like doing sport, traveling, and watching movies. I am also ambitious in life. Even if it can be perceived as a good or a bad trait, it kept me continuously on the right track from high school all the way through to the professional world.

In one word, I believe I can contribute to the performance of your company because I am a good analyst and an effective team player. Thank you, and apologies if I have been too long.

CASE 3: General Practitioner Position Interview (Low Experience)

Dear Members of the panel, thank you for the opportunity to have this interview and eventually work for your medical clinic as a General Practitioner.

My name is Steve Ramirez, 26 years old, and I am single. I graduated from the New York University School of Medicine last year. My thesis covered "Solid Digestive Cancers Prevention and Treatment" and received "Cum Laude mention" from the Jury. I loved medicine since my early childhood, and that is why I am stepping up today to become a General Practitioner.

I have got the opportunity to gain some experience while being in medical school. Since my fourth year, I enrolled to be an anatomy instructor for first- and second-year medical students. This experience allowed me to acquire a more reliable capacity to diagnose, coupled with a more profound understanding of physiology.

About the day-to-day work, I always perform my job with the highest standards to meet expectations. I research everything, and I always double-check my work, I communicate, and I respect hierarchy.

From my resumé, you can see my interest in topics related to medicine through the certifications I completed on nutrition, emergency health, and biostatistics. This is to give an overview of the technician I am.

As a person, I am easygoing, smiling, respectful, humble, open-minded, and easy to work with. I like doing sport, traveling, and hiking. I am also ambitious in life. Even if it can be perceived as a good or a bad trait, it kept me continuously on the right track all the way from high school to my doctoral studies.

In one word, I believe I can contribute to the performance of your medical clinic because I am a reliable practitioner and a friendly person. Thank you, and apologies if I have been too long.

CASE 4: Marketing Manager Position Interview (Experienced)

Dear Members of the panel, I appreciate the opportunity to sit and discuss how I can be a fit for the Marketing Manager position in your company.

My name is Catherine Sanders, and I am 32 years old. I am a marketing specialist by trade and training. There are five points that best describe me.

During my eight years of experience, I have worked in two different industries at the manager level. I have built a great deal of **sectorial competence** cutting across retail, household appliances, apparel, curation, and online shopping.

Functionally speaking, I have harnessed a range of skills that allowed me to exceed targets for seven years in a row. As we all know, a broad array of direct and indirect knowledge synergizes to make a good marketer. I mean, knowledge like psychology, copywriting, design, or strategic management. More specifically, for me, I have built robust competences in copywriting and strategic management, along with a good understanding of design and psychology.

The third point is that I have a **robust scorecard**. As I said earlier, I have exceeded targets for the last six years in a row. As a way of illustration, my targets included sales volume and amount, new account signups, brand awareness, new outlet openings, product listing count, or salesforce performance.

The next point is that, as a person, I am collaborative, focused, goal-oriented, autonomous, easy to work with, and very communicative. I'm an award-winning over-communicator [joke].

Last but not least, I have been closely following your company for the previous two years. My interest has grown because of the strong performances, coupled with a remarkable capacity to innovate. To be honest, I am not interviewing because I need a job, but because I believe in what you're are doing.

So, in one word, I am a consistent performer, and I believe in what you're doing. Thank you, and apologies for this lengthy introduction.

CASE 5: Finance Analyst Position Interview (Medium Experience)

Dear Members of the panel, I appreciate the opportunity to sit and discuss how I can be a fit for the Finance Analyst position in your organization.

My name is David Laporte, and I am 29 years old. I am an accountant by training. I'd like to introduce myself in five points.

During my short five years of experience, I have progressively built a wide spectrum of **sectorial competences**, cutting across corporate finance and public sector entities' financial management. I have leveraged my two job positions to become familiar with government projects finance, International organizations finance, and audit.

From a **functional perspective**, I have robust capabilities in financial reporting for both private and public sector entities, along with strong skills in budgeting, procurement, payables management, travel expenses management, reimbursable expenses recovery, and employee benefits, to name a few. I have been congratulated several times for the analytical orientation and readability of my financial reports. In addition to that, I have acquired intermediate to advanced skills in ERP softwares like SAP and SAGE.

The third point is that I have a **strong scorecard** progressively established through accountability and resourcefulness as a chartered accountant. I have received unqualified audits reports for three fiscal years in a row when managing funds for the government. I also received the "strong" internal control certificate last year for my job as an accountant for Health Project.

The next point is, as you have probably noticed on my resumé, that I have got a constant **interest in management related topics**. That's why I have completed the certification in accounting, coupled with data-driven decision making and business communication programs. The rationale is that when I learn to think like my manager, I do my job way better.

As a person, I am proactive and self-directed. I am also collaborative, result-oriented, and easy to work with. I like playing chess, football, and tennis.

In one word, I am a personally and critically committed accountant that is feeling ready to take up more challenges. Thank you, and sorry for this lengthy introduction.

Propose Value

⇒ Value Proposition for Products & Services

unique/ different/ true/ life-style/ passion	life/ freedom/ adventure/ no commitment	customized/ personal/ vintage	easy/ simple/ one time/ frictionless
faster/ instant/ quick / no time	affordable/ no cost/ cheap	one day/ one week/ one year	one-page/ one-place/ one-click
all/ complete/ total/ constant/ fixed/ stable	first/ best/ better/ leader/ world class	online/ on-demand/ web-based/ 24/7	local/ bio/ handmade/ natural
heal/ cure/ treat/ save/ shelter/ help	double/ triple/ 10x/ deal/ coupon/ promo	safety/ warranty/ protection	lifetime/ sustainable/ long term
performance/ effective/ efficient/ agile	grow/ improve/ develop/ certified	powerful/ resistant/ long lasting	result/ performance/ productivity
features/ benefits/ advantages	principles/ rules/ guidelines	fundamental/ essential/ comprehensive	solve problems/ give options
goals/ objectives / targets	steps/ ways/ process/ method	strategies/ techniques/ hacks	analytics/ trend/ keywords
data/ intelligence/ assessment	innovative/ breakthrough/ top notch	for everyone/ everywhere/ anytime	for intelligent/ dummies/ shy/ introvert
entrepreneur/ investor/ professional	for traveler/ developer/ executive	for men/ girl/ women	wealthy/ riche/ successful
beautiful/ elegant/ design/ classic	since 1899/ tradition/ history	globally recognized/ top/ gold	$billion/ $million/ $100K/ $10K

- **Dollar Shave Club**

    "A great shave for a few bucks a month. No commitment. No fees. No BS." (13)

- **Zoom**

    "Make video communications frictionless."

- **Stripe**

    "Web and mobile payments, built for developers."

- **MailChimp**

    "Send better emails."

- **Lyft**

    "Rides in minutes. Take the wheel."

- **Mizzen and Main**

    "Performance fabric. Traditional style."

- **Pagely**

    "We help the world's biggest brands scale and secure WordPress."

- **Bitly**

    "Shorten. Share. Measure."

- **Unbounce**

    "Build, publish & A/B test landing pages without I.T."

- **Apple MacBook**

    "Light. Years ahead."

- **FreshBooks**

    "Small business accounting software designed for you, the non-accountant." (14)

- **DuckDuckGo**

"The search engine that doesn't track you."

♘ Mint

"It's all coming together. When you're on top of your money, life is good. We help you effortlessly manage your finances in one place." (15)

♘ Weebly

"The easiest way to make a website. It's surprisingly easy to create your own website, blog or online store." (16)

♘ Tortuga Backpacks

"The best carry on travel bag."

♘ Opera

"Fast, secure, easy-to-use browser."

♘ TheLadders

"Highest paying job search. Join the #1 job search site for $100K+ jobs."

♘ Pinterest

"Discover recipes, home ideas, style inspiration and other ideas to try."

♘ Salesforce

"Connect to your customers in a whole new way with the world's #1 CRM platform." (17)

♘ Square

"The one-stop run-your-business shop. From payments to payroll, there are Square solutions for almost everything."

♘ Skype

"Free online calls, messaging, affordable international calling to mobiles or landlines and Skype makes it easy to stay in touch."

Uber

"Get a ride in minutes. Or become a driver and earn money on your schedule. Uber is finding you better ways to move, work, and succeed." (18)

Starbucks

"Let us treat you. Drink coffee, earn Stars, get Rewards."

Evernote

"Our note taking app helps you capture and prioritize ideas, projects and to-do lists, so nothing falls through the cracks." (19)

Hubspot

"The HubSpot growth platform lets your entire company work together -- from marketing, to sales, to customer service. Each product is powerful alone, but better together."

Spotify

"Spotify is a digital music service that gives you access to millions of songs. No credit card needed." (20)

Plated

"More great meals are on the way. Stay tuned, we'll be expanding our range of Plated cooking kits in the near future." (21)

Invision

"Design better. Faster. Together. The digital product design platform powering the world's best user experiences." (22)

Optimizely

"We're Optimizely. Nice to meet you. Optimizely is the world's leading experience optimization platform."

DeskBeers

"Business class drinks delivery. Craft and small-batch drinks delivered to offices."

- **GlassDoor**

"To help people everywhere find a job and company they love." (23)

- **ClassPass**

"The most flexible fitness membership ever. ClassPass is an all-access membership of 10,000 fitness studios. Try strength training, cycling and more."

- **Updatey**

"Simple. Beautiful. Project Management."

- **Apple**

"Think different. Tech that works. Your privacy is safe with us."

- **Google**

"Free search engine. Free tools and apps. Targeted text-based ads for businesses. Content monetization."

- **Amazon**

"Anything you want quickly delivered. Sell better, sell more. Easy to read on the go."

Sell Your Products

⇒ Attention

the best $xxx ROI ever	are you ready for the next [...]?	are ready to face [...]?
the best [...] created for you	no one wants to insure you	no one wants to listen to you
save money up to [..]% in your [..] today	are you still [...]?/ stop [...]	get a [..] for less than [..]

- 99 The best $xxx ROI ever.
- 99 No one wants to insure you.
- 99 No one wants to listen to you.
- 99 The best design created for you.
- 99 Stop buying expensive furniture.
- 99 Are you still competing on price?
- 99 Get a car for the price of a coffee.
- 99 Are you still realizing others' dreams?
- 99 Are you still buying expensive hosting?
- 99 Stop wasting time on business research.
- 99 Save up to 50% on your electricity bills.
- 99 Are you still hiring the wrong salespeople?
- 99 Are you ready for the next changes in tax law?

IMPRESS

- 💬 The best outsourcing solutions designed for you.
- 💬 Are you still repairing your plumbing every month?
- 💬 Are you prepared to survive the next economic downturn?
- 💬 Are you still struggling to make money out of your practice?
- 💬 Are you still spending hundreds of dollars on a book cover?
- 💬 Are you still struggling to find the best house for your family?
- 💬 Are you still paying people just to sit around and play crosswords?

⇒ Interest

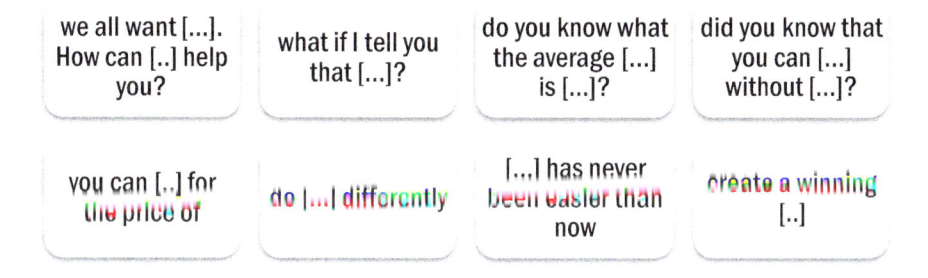

we all want [...]. How can [..] help you?	what if I tell you that [...]?	do you know what the average [...] is [...]?	did you know that you can [...] without [...]?
you can [..] for the price of	do [...] differently	[...] has never been easier than now	create a winning [..]

- 💬 Do your accounting differently!
- 💬 Selling online has never been easier.
- 💬 You can save forests without leaving your office!
- 💬 Create and execute a winning marketing strategy.
- 💬 You can learn storytelling for the price of a burger.
- 💬 We all want a carefree life. How can ABC help you?
- 💬 What if I tell you that you could make it 10X faster?

> What if I tell you that you could have all this in one click?

> We all want the best for our children. How can we help you?

> Do you know what the average time lost doing the old way is?

> We all want to hire the best. How can ABC help you make it?

> We all want to make the most of our spare time. How to do it?

> Do you know how much is wasted every day doing the old way?

> Do you know that this is actually costing you thousands of dollars?

> What if I tell you that your English level has reached a plateau?

> Do you know what your efficient customer acquisition cost should be?

> What if I told you that you can build your dream house in less than one month?

⇒ Desire

get all [...] for only [..]	now you can [...] without [..]	we take care of your [..] for you
all solutions in one bundle	one solution for all your [...]	now you can focus on [...]
fast-forward your career with [..]	it's the only [...] available	100% satisfaction guaranteed
you will never have this problem again	you will never [...] the same way	you will never have to worry about [...] again
thousands of companies like you have [...]	thousands of people like you are already using it.	grow your business/ [..] at your fingertips

IMPRESS

- All solutions in one bundle.
- 100% satisfaction guaranteed.
- We take care of your kids for you.
- One solution for all your payments.
- You will never have a bad start again.
- It's the fastest survey solution available.
- You will never do PR the same way again.
- All you need to run a successful company.
- Now you are free to work where you want.
- Thousands of companies have made the leap.
- You will never have to worry about delivery again.
- Thousands of people like you are already using it.
- Grow your business without growing your capacities.
- It's the only bank that pays you to open your account.
- Thousands of companies like you have made the shift.
- Fast-forward your career with a professional certification!
- Thousands of companies like you have adopted this solution.
- We take care of payroll so that you can focus on your real business.
- We take care of delivery, so you can focus on growing your business.
- We take care of CRM so that you can grow your business everywhere.

⇒ Action

get sarted for free	chose your plan/ order now	one last thing ...	get it for as low as [...]/this is a limited offer
It's at maximum value today	this offer expire in [...]	if you're not sure, try it for free.	buy now to get [..] free
early bird offer is only [..]	special offer for you	get a [..] bonus that is worth [..]	cancel a anytime
money back guarantee	request a quote	start your trial today	start learning today

- 💬 Try now.
- 💬 Enroll today.
- 💬 Cancel anytime.
- 💬 Request a quote.
- 💬 Choose your plan.
- 💬 Get a $70 gift in bonus.
- 💬 Buy now to save $1,100.
- 💬 It's at maximum value today.
- 💬 This offer expires in one week.
- 💬 If you're not sure, try it for free.
- 💬 The early bird offer is only $230.
- 💬 One last thing, you can try it with no engagement.
- 💬 30 Days money-back guarantee. No question asked.

- 💬 A special offer for you. Save $1,256 today on the full option.
- 💬 If you buy today, you will get a one-month subscription for free.
- 💬 Today you can have it for as low as $499. This is a limited offer.
- 💬 One last thing, you will receive a 20% discount if you order by October 19, 2019.

Pitch Your Project

⇒ Common Elements of a Pitch

Problem	Solution	Product / Service	Market Validation
Adoption Strategy	Business Model	Market Share	Financials
Competition	Competitive advantages	Scaling plan	Team

Box 2: The Psychology of Pitching

Your pitch should answer these three questions in a short time, usually less than 10 mins:

<u>Why will you succeed?</u>

- Problem – Solution - Product
- Market validation
- Adoption strategy
- Competitive advantages
- Scenarios

<u>What size is the opportunity?</u>

- Market share
- Business model
- Positioning
- Financials

<u>Who are you?</u>

- Competition
- Team

IMPRESS

CASE 6: AirBed&Breakfast's (AirBnB) Pitch Deck

SLIDE 1: Cover

AirBed&Breakfast

Book rooms with locals, rather than hotels.

AirBed&Breakfast

SLIDE 2: Problem

- **Price** is an important concern for travelers booking trips online.
- **Hotels** keep you disconnected from the city and its culture.
- **No easy way currently exists** to book a room with local or become a host.

SLIDE 3: Solution

A platform where users can rent out their space to host travelers to:

SAVE MONEY	MAKE MONEY	SHARE CULTURE
• when traveling	• when hosting	• local connection to the city

SLIDE 4: Market Validation

Couchsurfing.com   Craigslist.com

IMPRESS

660,000
Total Users

50,000
Temporary Housing Listings
per week in the US in San Francisco and New York City between 07/09 and 07/16

SLIDE 5: Market Size and Share

We target 10.6M trips booked online.

AirBnB Serviceable Available Market
- 10.6M (Trips)

Total Available Market
- 532M (Online Trips)
- 1.9 Billion + (Trips Booked Worldwide)

SLIDE 6: Product

A website where users can easily access:

SEARCH BY CITY   REVIEW LISTINGS   BOOKING

SLIDE 7: Business Model

We take a 10% commission fee on each transaction:

IMPRESS

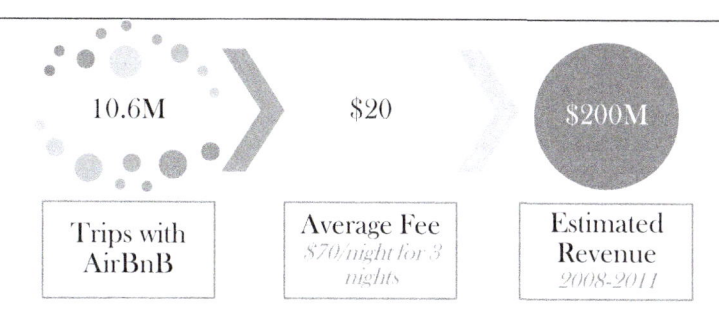

10.6M → **$20** → **$200M**

Trips with AirBnB	Average Fee	Estimated Revenue
	$70/night for 3 nights	*2008-2011*

SLIDE 8: Adoption Strategy

EVENTS

Target events monthly:
  Octoberfest (6M)
  Cebit (700K)
  Summerfest (1M)
  Eurocup (3M)
  Mardi Gras (800K)

PARTNERSHIPS

Cheap / alternative travel:
  Goloco
  Kayak
  Orbitz

CRAIGSLIST

Dual posting feature

SLIDE 9: Competition

AFFORDABLE

- CouchSurfing
- Craigslist
- BedandBreakfast.com

- AirBed&Breakfast
- Hostels.com

OFFLINE TRANSACTION | **ONELINE TRANSACTION**

- Rentobi.com
- VRBO

- Rentahome
- Orbitz
- Hotels.com

EXPENSIVE

SLIDE 10: Competition Advantages

1st TO MARKET
- for transaction-based temporary housing site

HOST INCENTIVE
- they can make money over couchsurfing.com

LIST ONCE
- hosts post one time with us vs. daily on craigslist

EASE OF USE
- search by price, location & check-in / check-out dates

PROFILES
- browse host profiles, and book in 3 clicks

DESIGN & BRAND
- memorable name will launch at historic DNC to gain share of mind

SLIDE 11: Team

Joe Gebbia,
User Interface & PR

- Entrepreneur and designer. Holds a patent for his product, CritBuns®. A graduate of the Fhode Island School of Design (RISD), has dual BFA's in graphic design and industrial design.

Nathan Blecharcyk,
Developer

- Created Facebook Apps "Your neighbors" (75,000 users) and "Rolodextrous", recently launched "Identified Hits". A graduate of computer science Harvard, Nate has worked at Microsoft, OPNET technologies, and Batiq.

Brian Chesky,
Business Development & Brand

- Founder of Brian Chesky, Inc, Industrial design consultant. A graduate of the Rhode Island School of Design (RISD), has a BFA in industrial design.

Michel Seibel, *Advisor*

Michel is the CEO and Co-founder of justin.tv, a San Francisco based venture-funded startup that delivers live video to the Internet.

IMPRESS

Box 3: 7 Golden Rules for Pitching

1. Be solving a problem – a *real one*.
2. Get your points across quickly – under 60 seconds.
3. Keep it simple to understand – *fifth-grade kid*.
4. Add simple images and diagrams – *circles, squares, and triangles*.
5. Show "big pictures" – *1 slide per point*.
6. Say often your unique, hard to copy differentiation momentum – *2+ times*.
7. Have the least possible assumptions – *one or less*.

CASE 7: UberCab's Pitch Deck

SLIDE 1: Cover

UberCab

Next-Generation Car Service.

[UBER logo]

SLIDE 2: Problem 1 - Cabs in 2008

Most use aging & inefficient technology

- Radio dispatch, no 2-way communication
- Most common car, Ford Crown Victoria = 14mpg

Hailing is done by hand or phone

- No GPS coordination between client/driver.
- Significant fare-seeking or "dead-time."

SLIDE 3: Problem 2 - Quality of service

Taxi-monopolies reduce quality of service.

Medallions are expensive, and drivers underpaid.

Medallions cost ~$500k, drivers make $31k.

No incentive / accountability for drivers / clients.

SLIDE 4: Solution – UberCab Concept

- A fast & efficient on-demand car service
- Market: Professionals in American cities
- The convenience of a cab in New York City (NYC) + experience of a professional chauffeur. But in San Francisco and NYC.
- Latest consumer web & device technology
- Automate dispatch to reduce wait-time
- Optimized fleets and incented drivers
- The "NetJets of car services."

IMPRESS

SLIDE 5: Product

UberCabs apps

- **1-Click** request from Geo-aware devices
- SMS from any phone **"pickup @work in 5"**

Must be a member to use the service	Not hailed from street	Guaranteed Pick-up (unlike a yellowcab)
• Professional and trustworthy clientele	• So no medallion licences are required, since clients are service members & use digital-hail	• Mobile app will match client & driver. See photos of each other

SLIDE 6: Product

UberCap.com

- Book Trips, show Fleet status, trip history
- Pre-specify locations with labels + coordinates to enable easy texting of pickup location
- Google Maps integration: Lat/long for "home," "bob-work," "alice-apt"

SLIDE 7: Competition Advantages

1-click hailing	Members only	Optimized fleet	Fast Response time
• "pickup here in 5 mins"	• Respectable clientele	• Logistical LBS software	• Easier than calling

	Luxury automobiles	High-tech solutions:	Great drivers	
	• Mercedes Sedans	• Geo-aware auto-dispatch	• "Rate your trip" feature	

147

IMPRESS

SLIDE 8: Operating Principles

- Luxury service on-demand
- Modern and fuel-efficient fleet
- Customer-focused, computer-coordinated
- The best end-user experience possible
- Statistically optimized response time
- Pre-paid, cashless billing system
- Profitable by design

SLIDE 9: Use-Cases

| Fast local transport where parking isn't easy | Trips to/from restaurants, bars & shows | Airport pickup/dropoff (pre-shceduled) | Working while commuting (wifi in cars) |

SLIDE 10: Benefits

- Cabs don't guarantee pickup and take 45 mins
- Cars aren't as safe or clean as limos
- Car services require 1-3 hours' notice
- Car services transfers average over $60 + tax
- UberCab would be faster & cheaper than a limo, but nicer & safer than a taxicab

IMPRESS

SLIDE 11: Initial Service Area

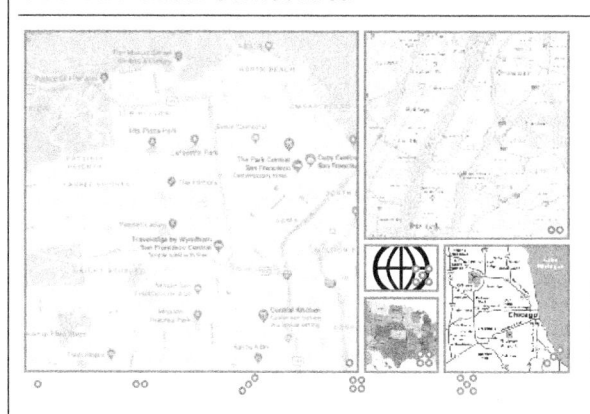

Central San Francisco, then Manhattan after ...

SLIDE 12: Technology

Mobile phone + intelligent scheduling
• Application for iPhone, Blackberry, Symbian Operations research for route optimization

Payment/ utilization/ reputation tracking

Pataent-pending system design

SLIDE 13: Demand Forecasting

Cars hover in statistically optimized positions

Minimized expected pickup time given hour of week weather / traffic conditions

IMPRESS

SLIDE 14: Overall Market

$4.2B
Annually and growing

22% of revenues. Top 4 players combined.

SLIDE 15: Composition of Market

Major Market Segments.

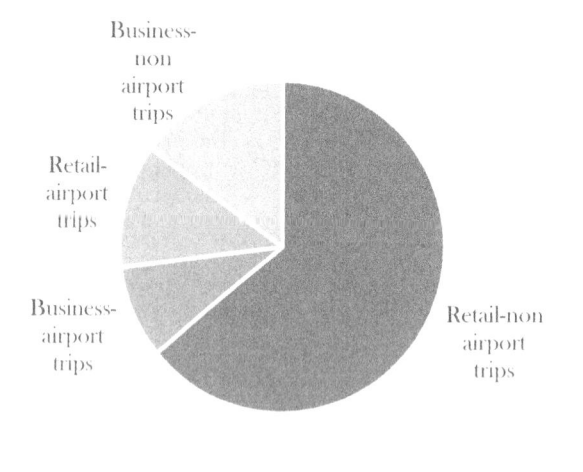

- Business-non airport trips
- Retail-airport trips
- Business-airport trips
- Retail-non airport trips

- 2007 Market
- Focus on Urban service on-demand

IMPRESS

SLIDE 16: Target Cities

Focus on San Francisco / New York City to begin

Expand to Los Angeles, Chicago, Houston, Pennsylvania, Dallas

This covers 50% of entire US market

SLIDE 17: Looking Forward

Potential Outcomes:

Best-Case Scenario:
- Becomes market leader, $1B+ in yearly revenue.

Realistic Success Scenarion
- Gets 5% of the top 5 US Cities. Genarates 20-30M+ per year profit.

Worst-Case Scenario
- Remains a 10 car, 100 client service in San Francisco (SF). Time-saver for SF based executives.

SLIDE 18: Looking Forward

Location-Based Services (LBS)

Extend infrastructure to other LBS applications
(Delivery, non-critical medical / governmental use)

$3.5B

Industry Size

• Growing to a 3.5B industry by 2010

SLIDE 19: Smartphone Operating Systems

Quarterly worldwide smartphone sales by OS vendor

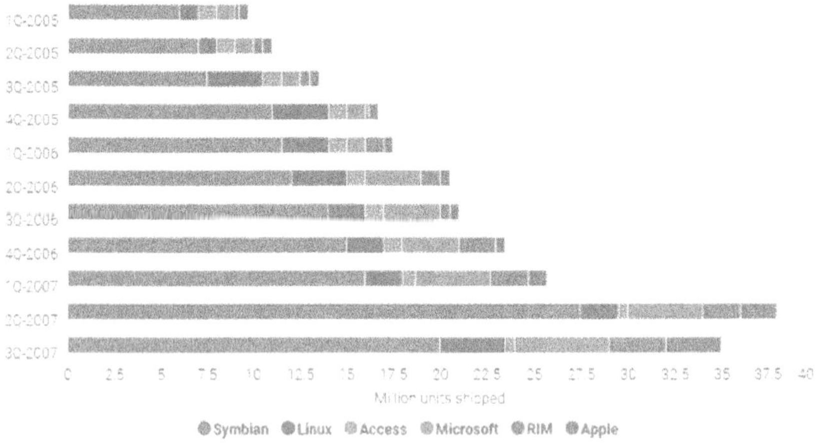
1Q-2005
2Q-2005
3Q-2005
4Q-2005
1Q-2006
2Q-2006
3Q-2006
4Q-2006
1Q-2007
2Q-2007
3Q-2007
0 2.5 5 7.5 10 12.5 15 17.5 20 22.5 25 27.5 30 32.5 35 37.5 40
Million units shipped
Symbian Linux Access Microsoft RIM Apple

(Source: Slidebean.com)

SLIDE 20: Smartphone Sales

IMPRESS

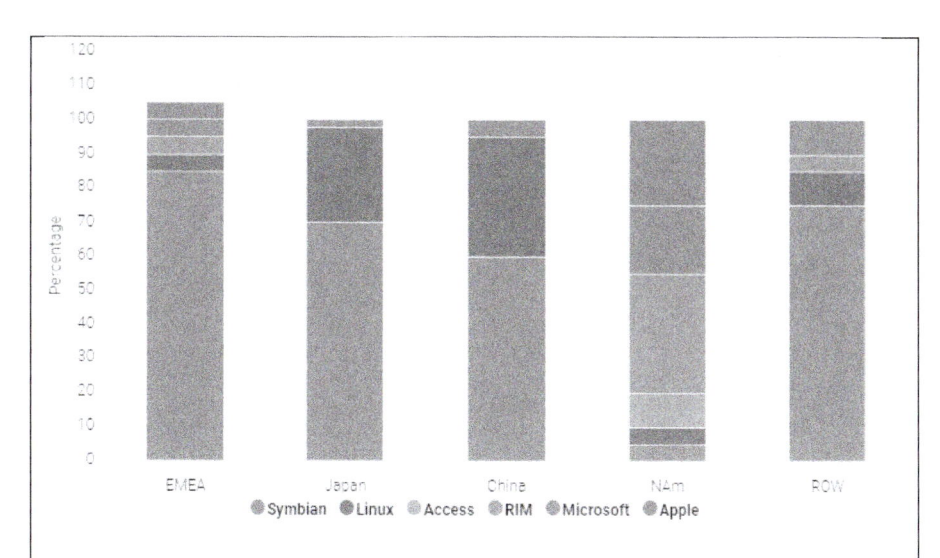

[Bar chart showing percentage by region: EMEA, Japan, China, NAm, ROW, with categories Symbian, Linux, Access, RIM, Microsoft, Apple]

(Source: SlideBean.com)

SLIDE 21: Future Optimizations

Pay premium for on-demand service

Get here "now" costs more than "tomorrow at 5pm"

Discounted rates for Sun-Tues multi-hour bookings

More accurate GPS technology

Cheaper cars by buying used

Less expensive hybrid vehicles (Prius)

SLIDE 22: Go-to-Market

Marketing Ideas

" *...The One-click cab*

...The NetJets of Limos

...Cabs 2.0

Possible slogans

Become the ubiquitous "premium" cab service

Invite only, referred from an existing member

YellowCab is the only recognizable brand

SLIDE 23: Traction

Progress to Date

- Ubercab.com reserved + "ubercab" SMS code
- California LLC + trademark filed
- iPhone dev license applied for Nov 28, 2008
- Bank Account + PayPal account created
- 5 advisors & 15 clients now recruited
- Provisional patent filed
- NEXT: buy 3 cars, develop an app, Feb. 1st demo

- Raise a few million, small-office + GM in SF

Advocate for Reforms

⇒ On Advocacy Terms

social policy	social reform	agenda building	policy advocacy
ecology of policy advocacy	welfare/wealth /solidarity	powerless populations	equality/ rights/ freedom
social justice/ death penalty	vulnerable populations	social communities	governmental setting
electoral setting	community setting	agency setting	policy analysis
policy analysis framework	existing / new policies	policy proposal	policy road map
problems and solutions	domestic problems	international factors	national/ global level
forces/ endorsement/ pressure	media coverage	decision-making	cynicism/ resistance
policy advocacy skills	policy-enacting task	effectiveness of operating programs	across national borders
diagnosis/ listening stage	softening/ moderating stage	early maneuvering	activating stage
strategies of persuasion	adversarial communication	friendly communication	struggle is raging

Box 4: 4 Styles of Policy Advocacy Practice

1. *Ballot-based Advocacy Style*

    You usually employ this style during political campaigns. As a policy advocate, you will work with political parties, campaign organizations, and campaign staff. Your capacity to frame issues and talk with voters will be determinant. Your ability to intelligently work with campaign staff will also be handy.

2. *Legislative Advocacy Style*

    In this advocacy style, your goal is usually to induce legislators to adopt a new measure or defeat an existing one. You will, therefore, work with trade and professional associations, unions, and lobbyists NGOs or organizations. The relevant capacities are policy analysis, lobbying, coalitions, and networking.

3. *Analytic Advocacy Style*

    In this style of advocacy, your goal is to carry out the evaluation of existing policies and then advocate change or end of these policies. To engage a successful analytical advocacy initiative, you will need proper research, data analysis, presentation, and communication skills. Without these skills, you will not be able to undertake a successful analytic advocacy engagement.

4. *Troubleshooting Advocacy Style*

    Why is it that a vital program is not effective? That's where you come in with the objective of increasing the effectiveness of existing operating programs. The main stakeholders you will work with are planning groups, insider and outside consultants, government officials, funders, consumers, and more. This style is not entirely based on analytics like the former one. Instead, what you will need are diagnosis, collaboration, and communication skills. (24)

- 💬 To me, this proposal is not based on any sound public **policy analysis**.
- 💬 I think we should avoid **adversarial communication** regarding this reform.
- 💬 We shall focus on **policy formulation** and **enactment**, planning, and implementation.
- 💬 When **developing policy proposals,** consultants and analysts take the environment into account.
- 💬 **Social reforms** like these do not have an immediate impact but are felt over a more extended period.
- 💬 The lessons learned from a central agency or larger department can be adapted to a **small agency setting**.
- 💬 The funds were used to execute programs under education, **social policy, advocacy,** and **communication.**
- 💬 The institution is intending to develop better strategies for communicating, **lobbying, and advocating**.
- 💬 The **ecology of policy advocacy** is composed of governmental, legislative, community, and agency settings.
- 💬 The key players in **government settings** could be political institutions, heads of government, or courts.
- 💬 The **policy options** have been identified and refined during the **diagnosis stage** of the water and sanitation sector.
- 💬 The task could be performed in less than fifteen minutes but will take longer if you extend it into an **agenda-building** session.

> The right thing to do now is to use the funds to engage in healthy eating promotion at home, at work, or in a **community setting**.

> Last year, the institution drastically reduced its international **policy advocacy** activities to focus its resources on urgent programs.

> The program has resulted in the development of a better **lobbying strategy** and the training of staff on effective **strategies of persuasion**.

> The government is having a **friendly communication** around the policy proposal. We are pretty much expecting adoption of the measure.

⇒ On Advocacy Actors

advocates/ policy advocates	bureaucrats/ local governments	mass media/ advocacy groups	legislative branches/ processes
executive branches	elected officials	unelected officials	liberals/ conservatives
courts/ legislators	standing committees	lobbyists/ interest groups	mindsets/ public opinion
political parties/ voters	campaign organizations	campaign staff	trade organizations
professional organizations	implementation team	planning groups	key players/ key officials

Box 5: 4 Rationales for Participating in Social Policy Advocacy (25)

- Ethical rationale
- Analytical rationale

- Political rationale
- Electoral rationale

⇒ On Advocacy Actions

commit to an issue	commit to problems	lobby for change/advocate for change	join a social reform
build policy/ build agendas	surmount cynicism	expand policy advocacy	analyze problems
frame issues	obtain data/ process data	conduct research	evaluate policies
develop policy proposal	make technical presentations	engage in ballot-based policy	troubleshoot and assess policies
develop political strategy	put into action	bring pressure on	build/sustain coalitions
develop links with advocacy groups	present policy proposals	defend policy proposals	gain support
build momentum	adopt a measure	defeat a measure	fight back

💬 Our country must **commit to** solving this pending cross-border **issue**.

💬 Several political forces are keeping actors from **joining this social reform**.

💬 We must **frame the issues** in a clear way for both the general public and experts.

159

- 💬 Based on these analyses, we can **build an agenda** for action in the months ahead.
- 💬 The team will help the organizations **develop policy proposals** to address the recommendations.
- 💬 The advocacy campaign has not been enough to **surmount the cynicism** at large in the general public.
- 💬 The team will **evaluate the policies** of different organizations to find good practices and ways of improvement.
- 💬 To guarantee better results in this project, we must advocate **for a change** in how success is measured and evaluated.
- 💬 The mass media will take the voices of marginalized citizens to decision-makers and **bring pressure on** them to make changes.
- 💬 When presenting children's marriage as a violation of their fundamental rights, the report seeks to **build momentum for change**.
- 💬 This communication will emphasize the need to **build coalitions between** parliamentarians and civil society organizations to improve the level of citizen engagement.

Box 6: Six-Step Advocacy Engagement Process (25)
1. Social problem analysis
2. Identification of relevant options
3. Comparison of compelling options
4. Drafting of proposals
5. Research of supporters and funders for proposals
6. Making key presentations

Exercises

1. "Problem," "Solution," and "Product" are separate parts of a pitch deck.
    a. True
    b. False

2. Which one is not a rationale for participating in social policy advocacy?
    a. Ethnical rationale
    b. Political rationale
    c. Electoral rationale

3. Please write your job interview introduction pitch for your preferred job position.

Chapter 4
NEGOTIATE

Everyone is a negotiator. Some of us know it and aim at better deals; others ignore it at their own expense.

NEGOTIATE

⇒ Approaches

culture-based style	negotiation framework	cross-culture behavior	American-style
Japanese-style	Chinese-style	principle	technique
style	tactic	standard	toolbox

⇒ Wrongs

bright-line morality	misstatement of fact	overt disrespect	lies
outright lies	deception	dishonesty	disrespect
taunt	white lies	falsehood	threat

⇒ Tips

good cop/ bad cop	golden parachute*	perceptual contrast	crown jewels defense*
Pac-Man defense*	scarcity	exclusivity	walk out
bluff	anchoring	social proof	consistency
reciprocation	rule of thumb	bargain	expiration
greenmail*	tender offer*	poison pill*	Proxy vote*

Corporate takeover

⇒ Attitude

confident	overconfident	bluffing	liar
blunt	disrespectful	arrogant	abrasive
impatient	condescen-ding	eye contact	credibility
ambiguity	position	stance	body language

On Agreement, Deal, or offer

agreement	final agreement	bargaining agreement	written agreement	deal
final deal	binding deal	mutually beneficial deal	talking point	offer/ bid
counteroffer / counterbid	final offer	final offer declaration	final offer pronounce-ment	obligation
binding obligation	commitment	binding commitment	resolution	contract
unit/ bundle price	variable/ fixed price	lump sum/ variable price	transaction costs	delay/ delivery/ reception
contingency	assumption	deadlock issue	sub-issue	negotiation session

NEGOTIATE

single session negotiation	n-round negotiation	limit/ ceilling/ treshold	limitation in time	limitation in money
limitation in authority	off-the-edge demand	provision	legally-binding	non-essential terms
proposal	trap/ pitfall/ bait	forward-looking statement	trigger penalty	sunk costs/ irrelevant costs

- This part of the paragraph met with **general agreement**.
- The negotiating team accepted our **proposal** unanimously.
- The **agreement** shall be of unlimited duration as discussed.
- The **agreement** shall be of limited scope as explained earlier.
- I quite understand your concern about this paragraph of the **proposal**.
- I'm afraid this part of the paragraph doesn't meet with the **general agreement**.
- I am optimistic that we will reach a **mutually beneficial agreement** with your company.
- The other beneficiaries will, by a **written agreement**, waive their right to more extensive compensation.
- An **agreement** with the relevant stakeholders is necessary to establish the appropriate program structures.
- The other parties must, by a **written agreement**, waive their right to additional damages that may crop up in the future.
- We asked the counterpart negotiating team if they were still **in agreement** with the proposal, and they accepted it unanimously.

99 **Provisions** must be made in the **ABC agreement** on how the necessary information can be provided without violating non-disclosure terms.

On Your Negotiating Team

negotiating team	ethical negotiator	unethical negotiator	principled negotiator
bargaining power	negotiating power	collaborative negotiator	binding authority
negotiator	intermediary	authority	principal
mediator	bystander	have deal making skills	deal making acumen

- No third party, nor intermediate is involved in the deal.
- Facing this **bargaining power**, we could not raise the prices.
- This team is known for its **deal-making skills** in acquisitions.
- You must keep any information out of the sight of **bystanders**.
- We will not stand as **collaborative negotiators** this time around.
- I am confident in the deal-making skills of this negotiating team.
- Our private equity specialists have quite strong **deal-making skills**.
- The team will have **binding authority** for these negotiation rounds.
- I'm afraid I don't believe in the **deal-making skills** of the current team.
- If we fail to reach an agreement, a **mediator** is likely to be nominated.
- Without a great deal of information, our team will not have enough **bargaining power**.
- Intellectual property negotiations involve strong but flexible **deal-making acumen**.

- 💬 We are understood to be **ethical negotiators** because we are operating under public funding.

- 💬 We will need a **team with a great deal of expertise and experience** in intellectual property negotiations.

- 💬 You will not build **deal-making skills** overnight. You need to be beating on the craft for a specific time to make it.

- 💬 I don't care how secure are your **deal-making skills.** I want you to do your homework before the negotiation rounds begin.

- 💬 Your **deal-making skills** alone will not get you VC funding for your startup unless it is a quite attractive investment opportunity.

- 💬 The management of a VC firm involves having **flexible deal-making acumen,** which is hard to translate into written rules and guidelines.

On the Counterpart

negotiating team	bargaining power	negotiating power	have deal making skills
cede/ give in	counterpart	target	client
other side	mediator	buyer	seller
customer	lawyer	labor union	competitor

- The target is understood to be an **ethical negotiator**.
- I'm afraid we are ceding too much in the deal with **the client**.
- Our private equity specialists have quite strong **deal-making skills**.
- The team will have **binding authority** for these negotiation rounds.
- This other side is known for its **deal-making skills** in intellectual property.
- You must prepare any information concerning the **target** for the **negotiating team**.
- If we fail to reach an agreement with **the competitor**, a **mediator** is likely to be nominated.
- The labor union possesses significant **deal-making acumen** to snatch some more perks.
- Their team has a **great deal of expertise and experience** in intellectual property negotiations.
- **Being simply blunt** doesn't mean you have great deal-making skills nor the contrary. It all depends on the outcome.

On Reactions

force the hand of the	statement/mistatements	tough negotiation point	counteroffer
trigger penalty	put the kibosh on the deal	last-minute hesitation	objection
complaint	concession	indecision	hesitation
trust	move	indifference	stiff resistance

- 💬 This claim will be a **tough negotiating point** for us.

- 💬 We are not going to consider this **statement** as it is **forward-looking**.

- 💬 We will be forced to find another supplier **if no agreement could be reached**.

- 💬 We need to have something up and running by July. Otherwise, we will **trigger penalty**.

- 💬 Unfortunately, your offer is too low. It is not acceptable. We can only propose a **counteroffer** of $5.5 million.

- 💬 Can you provide the relevant documentation to support your **statement** on the valuation of the machinery?

- 💬 By trying to **force the hand of the commission**, you have taken unnecessary risks to **put a kibosh on the deal**.

- 💬 The expert will give you examples of conditions and events that may indicate the existence **of material misstatements**.

- 💬 The negotiating team isn't making any progress. Although, I don't think **forcing the hand** of the union is a good idea.

- 💬 We need to have the documentation on all **forward-looking statements** to see how the expert came to these figures.

- 💬 Our essential objective is to **force the hand of the founder** to apply lean management methods after the approval of the project.

- 💬 With all the risks and uncertainties, we cannot place undue reliance on **forward-looking statements** as a prediction of actual results.

- 💬 In a David against Goliath configuration like this one, you can **force the hand of the other side** to reach an agreement more rapidly.

- 💬 We have seen how, in the Tech project, the private equity firm managed to **force the hand of the team** to bring performance back.

- 💬 We will inquire about the audit reports to obtain reasonable assurance that the financial reports are **free from material misstatements**.

On Actions

make an offer	get the deal done	fail to reach an agreement	have a substantial leg up
impose consequences for misstatements	prepare properly ahead of time	disrupt counterpart's strategies	break negotiations down
reach an agreement	harness deal-making skills	do in-session research	force the hand of someone
postpone negotiations	file lawsuits against	trigger penalty	be defrauded
kill the deal	strike a deal	request supporting document	have a leg up
mislead	have deal making skills	put the kibosh on the deal	appraise/ accept/ reject

💬 We have a couple of observations regarding your **offer**.

💬 Our **offer is based on** the data collected from official sources.

💬 I am confident that we'll **get the final deal done** with the client.

💬 This piece of information will **disrupt the counterpart's strategy**.

💬 I quite understand your arguments, but we **can't accept** this **offer**.

💬 Your **offer** is pretty much what I was expecting, so I think we have a deal.

💬 We need **to reach an agreement** on the proposals as soon as possible.

💬 We will be **making an offer** only based on your documented statements.

- Our strategy for preventing outright lies is to **impose consequences for misstatements**.
- It is necessary to **properly prepare** the ground **ahead of time** for future negotiation rounds.
- If we were to reveal all the rejections we had, the VC would have **a leg up on** the capital to invest.
- If we were to reveal our actual costs, the clients would **have a substantial leg up** on our pricing.
- If **we fail to reach an agreement**, negotiations will **break down** and be **postponed** to our next fiscal year.
- **If no agreement is reached**, we will be filing lawsuits to claim compensations for material damages.
- We are pretty much abreast of these indirect benefits, but it doesn't change our **position about your offer**.
- **Negotiations broke down** last year and were **postponed** until the next rounds in the upcoming quarter.
- Before starting negotiations and **making a deal** with a VC, you always have to consult with your team.
- The administrator should **make an offer** of compensation after having considered the counterpart's arguments.
- The negotiations broke down when an **agreement could not be reached** on cost-sharing and waste management.
- I quite appreciate the size and cachet of the house, but I'm afraid your **offer** is not acceptable for that neighborhood.
- This is an **oversized proposal** regarding the project we are considering. You will need to work out a **smaller offer**.

- 💬 You, as Silicon Valley VCs, **have a leg up** in the tech startup world as you have already established your brands and leadership.

- 💬 If we were to reveal procurement methods, such as how the raw material was obtained, the competitors would **have a leg up** on our strategy.

- 💬 **Negotiations broke down** and were postponed until the next rounds in 2020 because the client made a compelling demand for a local factory building.

- 💬 **If no agreement is found**, then we reserve the right to seek remedies and damages to the fullest extent permitted by law. This will also include criminal prosecution.

- 💬 Really, we need to cut corners as a result of hectic schedules. This is the only offer we are going to make. You take it or leave it. We aren't **forcing your hand** either.

- 💬 If we were to reveal investigation methods, such as how the information was collected, the terrorist organizations would **have a leg up** on our military defenses.

- 💬 While the Japanese, German, and American firms **have a leg-up on us**, we are convinced that the solar cells produced by our firm can position us as a major supplier to the world market.

Exercises

1. To have a substantial leg up means:
   a. To have a higher bargaining power
   b. To close the deal
   c. To bluff

2. Why should you force the hand of the counterpart?
   a. To make a deal faster
   b. To put the kibosh on the deal
   c. To kill the deal

3. Which strategy is not useful to prevent outright lies?
   a. To impose consequences for misstatements
   b. To ask for documentation on all forward-looking statements
   c. To force the hand of the counterpart

Chapter 5
DESCRIBE

Choose your words wisely.

Describe Your Performance and Scorecard

⇒ Qualify Outstanding Performance

exceptional	unprecedented	unparalleled	remarkable	outstanding
phenomenal	extraordinary	fantastic	unrivalled	innovative
prodigious	unsurpassed	without precedent	singular	peerless
unusual	first time	one-of-a-kind	uncommon	as never before
record-breaking	great/ top	unique/ rare	unheard-of	unexampled
impressive	tremendous	astonishing	amazing	ground-breaking

DESCRIBE

⇒ Qualify Average Performance

average	satisfactory	satisfying	acceptable	passable
sufficient	respectable	adequate	reasonable	justifiable
appropriate	eligible	correct	all right	decent
mean	creative	collaborative	good	okay
valid	fair	OK	fine	safe

⇒ Qualify Poor Performance

appalling	disastrous	cataclysmic	devastating	detrimental
calamitous	terrible	adverse	inadequate	insufficient
inferior	unsatisfactory	dissatisfactory	unsatisfying	less than average
substandard	disappointing	disillusioning	unexpected	mediocre
lamentable	insignificant	trivial	inconsiderable	minor
minimal	narrow	petty	short	miserable
sparse	limited	deficient	failing	poor
small	tiny	meager	worthless	scanty

DESCRIBE

⇒ Describe Your Performance

coordinated closely with stakeholders	achieved the impossible under pressure	made the key decisions to resolve	brought performance back	met profit goals for x year
met sales objectives in x market	undercut competitors on x segment	preserved business continuity	exceeded targets consistently	overseen $millions projects
brought out the best of a team	took swift actions autonomously	provided fast, effective actions	tackled impossible things	provide expanded guidance
made good progress in hard times	had a good track record	led shattering reforms	had impressive accomplishm.	brought higher performance
made a breakthrough	achieved astonishing results	been highly effective in negotiations	delivered the promise under pressure	been long-term focused
had a short-term focus	generated dramatic improvements	had unprecedented success	won the crowning achievement	succeeded when all else failed
found a last resort solution	made disproportionate impact	built in a scalable fashion	worked in a coordinated fashion	performed in an integrated fashion
grown in a structured fashion	delivered in a timely fashion	led in a decentralized fashion	drawn reports/memorandums	performed in a consistent fashion
integrated in an orderly fashion	negotiated in Western fashion	achieved modest success	had terrible performance	resulted in spectacular failure
produced poor performance	had appalling performance	failed miserably	considered to be doomed to failure	turned out to be a recipe for disaster

179

DESCRIBE

Box 7: Top 5 Reasons Why Startups Fail

- Too many unproven assumptions
- Focus on the product rather than customers
- Failure to deliver the promise
- High production costs
- Insufficient funding to iterate enough

⇒ Choose Your Incremental Objectives

drive incremental value	drive incremental volume	drive incremental growth	drive incremental sales	deliver incremental value
add incremental value	provide incremental value	on an incremental basis	capture incremental gains	in an incremental way
in an incremental fashion	in an incremental manner	incremental approach	strong incremental growth	small incremental gains
incremental target	incremental goals	incremental result	incremental objectives	incremental market share
incremental traffic	incremental quality	incremental revenue growth	incremental change	incremental amount
incremental increase	incremental knowledge	incremental innovation	incremental development	incremental improvement
incremental production	incremental exposure	incremental risk	incremental reforms	incremental capacity

DESCRIBE

| incremental gains | incremental benefits | incremental budgeting | incremental funding | incremental working capital |

| incremental cash flow | incremental investment | incremental cost | incremental expenditures | incremental expenses |

DESCRIBE

Words for Recruiters

⇒ Find Competencies and Capabilities

is an effective team player	has forward thinking	is determined/ is focused	is long term focused
harnesses structured thinking	is critically committed	is personally committed	is passionate/ has passion for
has business acumen and judgement	has drive/ has motivation	has incredibly valuable skills	is resilient/ is consitent
has great sales skills	has successful track record	has incredibly important skills	is well versed in financial regulation
has leadership skills	has strong conceptual skills	has x years of experience in product design	demonstrates strong strategic skills
demonstrates strong analytical skills	has creative problem solving skills	demonstrates good commu. skills	demonstrates strong commu. skills
has x year of experience in manufacturing	deploys a personable approach	has an outgoing personality	has awareness and sensitivity about

DESCRIBE

produces excellent written communications	has exceptional interpersonal skills	possesses technological know-how	demonstrates industry know-how
participates in know-how sharing	has the necessary preconditions	has a good working knowledge of	is flexible/ demonstrates flexibility
has monitoring and reporting skills	has program management competencies	has a great deal of knowledge	is able to learn and adapt quickly
is able to fit in quickly	is willing to learn the business	has a sense of urgency	has a sense of commitment
has a sense of ownership	has a sense of purpose	has knowledge and expertise for	has advanced knowledge
communicates effectively	has a wide range of knowledge	shows respect for diversity	has know-how and expertise
possesses technical know-how	has the capacity to bring innovation	collaborates inclusively	has a set of relevant skills
has strong knowledge	has extensive knowledge	has working knowledge	has a strong knowledge base
realizes knowledge transfer	has core competences	is smart and motivated	has intercultural competencies
has professional competencies	realizes a transfer of competencies	has a good knowledge	has a great deal of knowledge
shows a lack of understanding	shows a lack of knowledge	is good at problem solving	has good people skills
is knowledgeable/ is highly qualified	is highly involved	has good insights	leads by example

183

DESCRIBE

⇒ Positive Traits

easy to work with	easy to talk to	have a gift for something	have a natural knack for	open minded
professional	proactive	intelligent	sensible	efficient
disciplined	alert	adaptable	organized	talented
skillful	creative	diplomatic	cooperative	industrious
resourceful	analytical	focused	ambitious	persuasive
confident	persistent	dogged	inspirational	bold
brave	courageous	responsible	wise	influential
adventurous	appreciative	observant	idealistic	imaginative
empathetic	enthusiastic	happy	funny	friendly
easygoing	kind	spontaneous	optimistic	passionate
extroverted	charming	tolerant	honest	trustworthy
extroverted	charming	tolerant	honest	trustworthy
loyal	gentle	just	simple	humble
low-keyed	discreet	patient	generous	courteous
independent	objective	supportive	traditional	unselfish
mature	calm	hospitable	meticulous	sophisticated
introverted	private	cautious	protective	thrifty/frugal

⇒ Negative Traits

disorganized	scatterbrained	inattentive	forgetful
evasive	impulsive	irresponsible	know-it-all
nervous	pessimistic	naive	gullible
dishonest	disloyal	spoiled	lazy
childish	irresponsible	greedy	pretentious
extravagant	impulsive	oversensitive	self-indulgent
rebellious	reckless	tactless	abrasive
stubborn	controlling	nagging	violent
grumpy	off-putting	mischievous	humorless
antisocial	compulsive	superstitious	paranoid
suspicious	nosy	manipulative	obsessive
insecure	whiny	possessive	resentful
self-destructive	cowardly	cynical	selfish
stingy	unethical	unintelligent	uncooperative
uncommunicative	materialistic	frivolous	hypocritical
sluggish	jealous	fussy	awkward
sheepish	hostile	haughty	evil

DESCRIBE

Words for Work

⇒ Expressions to Use for Activities

launch activities	launch a campaign	mobilize resources	look for sponsors	build new partnerships
call a meeting/ have a talk	have a workshop	have a brainstorming session	put off/cancel/ reschedule	communicate / delagate
day in and day out/ everyday	cover in more details	cover details/ nuts and bolts	assess the current situation	upstream actions
downstream actions	under communication	over communication	results-based management	work around the clock
where do we stand on [...]	leeway/ free hand/ autonomy	gap/ discrepancy/ difference	contingent/ depending	work stream/ workflow
share insights	client input/ feedback	judgment call/own view	sidetrack/ digress/ distract	sit on the fence/ be neutral

DESCRIBE

delivarables/ results	call it a day	hammer something out/ fight	flooded with new ideas	make new choices
connect with clients	grab more attention	take a actions/ hit the ground	discuss scenarios/ options	courses of action
hit the wall/ stop	clinch/ win hardly	hit the high points	avoid common pitfalls	hold accountable
take responsibility	take up challenges	operations/ budget/ resources/	segment/ niche/ category	execution/ implementation
agenda/ schedule/ meeting	beat around the bush/ lose focus	charge code/ budget	overspending /budget overrun	disbursement rate

⇒ Expressions to Use for Non-Profit Organizations

vision/ mission	leader/ leadership/ hierarchy	approach/ strategy	inclusion/ inclusive	sustainable/ resilient
welfare/ well being	transparent/ fair	effect/ impact	social innovation	justice/ death penalty
raise awareness/ sensitize	disadvantaged population	high net worth individual	bridge the gap/ close the gap	defend values
recipients/ beneficiaries	sensitize/ advocate	stakeholders/ actors	take into account	consider/ address
needs/ concerns	problems/ issues	dangerous conditions	precarious conditions	low wages/ low income

DESCRIBE

middle class	capacity reinforcement	youth/ young people	tackle/ respond	vulnerable population
needy population	deprived population	marginalized population	minorities/ inclusion	displaced population
shared prosperity	maldistribution of wealth	maldistribution of income	gender equality	gender inequality
wealth inequality	extreme poverty	income inequality	share of wealth	deep pocket/ superrich
equal pay/ wages	tackle inequality	challenge inequality	rules of engagement	instrument/ mechanism
social reforms/ advocacy	equal access to	grab more attention on	grapple with/ deal with	address issues/ tackle issues

DESCRIBE

⇒ Context Expressions to Use

we are in the midst of a crisis	in the face of uncertainty	displaced populations	low rainfall/ drought	economic crisis/slump
upheaval/war /conflict/ social stir	bushfire crisis	state of emergency	growing criminality	lack of alignment/ consistency
inadequate framework/ policy	poor system & procedures	low commitment	utterly new and frightening	cannot be more critical
lose control of a situation	get out of hand	received ideas/ cliché	be on the horns of a dilemma	on the edge of bankruptcy
run behind schedule	established patterns	price war/ declining sales	shrinking market share	shrinking profit
scandal/ allegations	growing competition	highly fragmented market	market trend/global trend	account for/ explain
deal a blow/cause failure	change in customers' need	competitor breakthrough	how monumental is the mountain to climb?	

DESCRIBE

⇒ Challenge Expressions to Use

highest priority	committment /engagement	challenges that tomorrow will bring	lower the curve	restore dignity
cost control/ risk control	kill costs/ downsize	accelerate growth	accelerate investments	organic growth
reduce carbon footprint	return to profitability	return to growth	return to stability	become profitable again
positioning/ repositioning	reduce exposure	disclose all risks	mitigate risks	increase capacity
quickly recover from the crisis	reduce customer attrition	commitment to customers	how to serve more customers	create a culture of excellence
hire the best people	solve problems efficiently	attain a critical mass	make better choices	get back on track
raise awareness	engage structural reforms	return to dialog	reduce the learning curve	make quick wins

190

DESCRIBE

⇒ Actions Expressions to Use

Take Action

grapple with/ deal with	get to grips with/ resolve	cope with/ handle	upstream work	downstream work
work around the clock	get the big picture	find key drivers/ forces	prioritize/ set forth	build a team/ delegate
speak effectively	sell an idea/ raise funds	kill an idea on the spot	build new partnerships	data-driven decision making
brainstorming/ solve creatively	focus all efforts	address a massive market	get a head start	get ahead of the game
win ahead/ start early	deploy our system	build our infrastructure	get things going	work hard every step
take to the next level	roll back/ withdraw	bounce back/ get back to normal	tailor according to specific needs	create incentive schemes

DESCRIBE

coach/ train/ share	shift to cloud computing	wrap your head around	encapsulate your thoughts	capture the essence of
analyze/ structure	develop hypothesis	discuss options	negotiate/ strike a deal	nail something down
take a step forward	challenge/ compete	take advantage/ harness	leverage capabilities	leverage resources
seize opportunities	put pressure	put your foot down	act decisively	communicate better
communicate transparently	cut corners/ cut cost	cut-off/ reduce	reach out to/ contact	put forth/ propose

Make Changes and Adjustments

change the way we are doing things	stay up to date on developments	delegate/ organize	shift focus from	adjust agenda
report progress	report regress/report problems	make adjustments	make arrangements	review and adapt the steps
learn and adapt	seek a new beginning	range of/ wide range of	plenty of/ variety of	several/ numerous
have room for improvement	share your view	it's a dead end	no hope of success	it is easily said than done
it's not a given	there is a long way to go	we are not out of the woods	adapt to new circumstances	stay private/ go public

DESCRIBE

Monitor and Follow Up

where do we stand on [...]?	control/ check	monitor/ follow up	follow through	follow up/ update
keep tabs on/ monitor	keep informed	evaluate/ assess	evaluate progress	report progress/ report regress
report solid results	assess risks/ risk exposure	assess the current situation	identify problems/ identify risks	communicate problems
reporting/ minutes/ note	make a survey/focus group	trace/ keep track	measure/ test	remove bottlenecks
gather/ collect	approve/ reject	keep an eye on	keep an eye out for	keep things going
evaluate impact	focused on the wrong things	monitoring & evaluation	evaluation memorandum	have the best evaluator
make recommendations	validation workshop	validation report	make a checklist	review/ check/ appraise
identify warning signs	we are running late	we run behind schedule	we are lagging behind	you are tilting at windmills

DESCRIBE

⇒ Results Expressions to Use

Set and Achieve Goals

achieved strategic goals	met objectives with tight resources	made good progress under uncertainties	increased market share by x%
won the early market the startup	won the mainstream market of the startup	achieved high-impact results	had a great track record for x years in a row
made a leap from X to Y	made a giant step in the X process	carried out all the planned activities	worked out significant results
performed complex data analytics for clients	handled acute situations autonomously	delivered beyond expectations	gained a great deal of experience
handled market penetration challenges	brought several incidents under control	built momentum for long term growth	mitigated operational risks

DESCRIBE

collaboratively	reduced exposure to natural disasters	transferred higher risks when necessary	eliminated risk by shifting to X technology
created profitable new products	created great products that hit it big in the market	created disruptive products	got customers to patronize the company
realized successful product launches	increased company valuation by $x million	achieved a consistent growth rate	created many revenue streams
analyzed sales data for decision making	secured higher margins	developed an optimum pricing model	broke even and turned profitable
performed cost-benefit analysis for decision making	grew a large customer base in x years	received have positive client feedback	built new technologies for automation
	analyzed adoption curve for decision making		

195

DESCRIBE

Define Problems

⇒ Qualify the Situation

in the wrong place at the wrong time	go down in flames/ fail spectacularly	a bad hair day/ a fate worse than death	one thing after another/ a vicious circle
in dire straits/ a perfect storm	out of the frying pan into the fire	trouble is brewing	a heavy cross to bear
when the shit hits the fan	it's not my day/ be stuck/ be in a hole	a snowball's chance in hell *(no chance)*	the crux of the matter *(the central element)*
be grasping at straws *(desperate)*	when it rains, it pours *(all at once)*	there are clouds on the horizon	confusing/ complicated/ baffling
appalling/ catastrophic/ disastrous	stormy/ hairy/ herculean	severe/ dire/ stiff/ strenuous	intricate/ insoluble/ opaque
serious/ tough/ problematic	uphill/ annoying/ tricky	last resort/ last chance	pressing/ uncertain/ uneasy
in the face of uncertainty	moving quickly/ outbreak	escalating/ intensified/ exacerbated	desperate/ hopeless/

DESCRIBE

- The Coronavirus outbreak is **moving quickly**.

- That situation, for many people, will be a **fate worse than death**.

- The food insecurity problem is exacerbated by a **severe drought**.

- The populations who are affected by the sinister are truly **in dire straits**.

- We are making this decision as a **last resort measure** to get out the storm.

- The Coronavirus outbreak is **serious** because the death toll is **rising quickly**.

- The company will **go down in flames** if the **opaque** transactions are made public.

- My apologies once again for the **wretched** technical problems we have at this end.

- The company is not doing well is this moment. I think **there are clouds in the horizon**.

- The impeachment doesn't have a **snowball's chance in hell** of passing at the Congress.

- To be honest, we somehow jumped **out of the frying pan into the fire** in terms of leadership.

- These days, if you are **in the wrong place at the wrong time**, you will be branded as a terrorist.

- When making decisions **in the face of uncertainty**, you are likely to be paralyzed by over-analysis.

- The government **is grasping at straws** and trying to find ways to avoid having Congress vote on this important bill.

DESCRIBE

❾ Harry Markopolos is the whistleblower who warned the public that **trouble was brewing** in Bernard Madoff's wealth management business.

DESCRIBE

⇒ Problems Expressions

a human tragedy	uphill battle/ quagmire	too high/ too low	increasing incertainties
worst-case scenario	gradually reaching limits	not feasible given constraints	trapped in/ trapped between
decline/ dwindle/ shrink	significant disruption	pressing issues/ alarming issues	collapse/ bankrupt/ fail
deeply concerned/ preoccupied	in trouble/ crisis/ nightmare/ hell	situation/ challenge/ issue/ problem	deeply challenging and unpredictable
magnitude of/ scope of/ level of	numbers go from bad to catastrophic	affecting/ reducing/ increasing	high tax level/ high prices/ high costs
underspending/ overspending	increased/stiff competition	price war/ dumping/ deregulation	increasingly difficult/ complex
critical/ untenable situation	serious/ recurrent problem	existing/ pending/ old/ new problems	the situation is preventing from
low level of/ low amount of	low budget/ low resources	customer attrition	conversion rate/ adoption rate
gather the numbers and facts	get the facts/ numbers	wrap your mind around the situation	wrap your head around the situation
capture the situation	walk someone through one's thoughts	select the preferred solution	mitigate a risk/ issue
gain time/ save time	get out of hand/ get out of control	cross the chasm/ bridge the gap	get through a situation

DESCRIBE

| get things underway | cut across all/ escalate | could be a distraction | consume precious resources |

| turn to your adavntage | solve a problem/ situation | the problem still prevails | the problem is growing |

⇒ Situation, Challenge, Issue

- In this situation, what is your problem definition?
- This situation imposes a significant **disruption** to the work.
- I want **the numbers and the facts**, not opinions nor feelings.
- Can you quickly gather **the numbers and facts** about this issue?
- What do we know precisely about **the magnitude of** the damages?
- **This issue is preventing** the company from getting the project underway.
- The case underway is a decline in revenue that no one can explain at this time.
- **This situation** can be explained by external and internal factors **affecting revenue**.
- The growth challenges are compounded by high tax levels and increased competition.
- There are significant changes in the market, and this **situation might worsen** as a result.
- To **solve this issue**, we'll need to use a clear approach and break it down into actionable items.
- In this situation, you need someone on the team who can bring DevOps experience to the table.
- Let's capture the situation by pinning down the problem definition before going forward with the case.

DESCRIBE

- Would you mind if I take a minute just to gather my thoughts and **wrap my mind around the situation**?
- When it comes to the **problem definition**, you need to recap the major points that encapsulate your thoughts.
- **The challenge is** that the team was short-handed from day one and needs to cut corners to meet the deadlines.
- The objective is to help the CEO of the company **get through this situation** by bringing sales and profitability back.
- Let me walk you through **my thoughts around this issue**: I want to look at the short-term and long-term opportunities for growth available to your company.

⇒ There Is A Problem That

- **There is** a governance **problem** that cuts across all this.
- **There is** a communication **problem that** cuts across all of this.
- **There is a problem** that no capacity reinforcement has been made for the teams in years.
- **The problem is these** branch management units suck. We'll find a politically correct way to put it.
- You need to adopt a broader view of **existing problems and issues** cutting across the portfolio.
- The increasingly difficult and untenable situation faced by employees is now **a serious problem**.
- **The problem is** a lack of coordinated international standards for public sector entities' financial management.
- The influential effect of the internet and technology will cut across all sectors, and the **problem is that** you seem to ignore it.
- The office has also noted that **there is a problem** with the electrical circuit, but this problem can only be fixed when we are not working.

DESCRIBE

- This year, however, **there is** an urgent **problem** that we should be aware of: we must produce more efficiently, or we are going to end up in trouble.

- **The problem is that** the program does not evaluate subjective criteria such as the speed of operation, customer support, or brand perceived value.

- The agreement that **there is a problem** and, therefore, a need for a new approach to enterprise architecture will allow for more effective organizational behavior.

- If **there is a problem** with our travel policy that does not allow the payment of these fees, then we should be fixing that problem rather than planning the next steps.

- In this regard, **there is a problem that** should be highlighted: in order to test the product, it is necessary to have a relevant sample from potential early adopters.

- **There is a problem**, however, **that** New Drug Project could be an enormous distraction, consuming precious resources in an area in which Pharma Client has little core capability.

⇒ Too Low

- The estimated revenue stream from this new product is **too low**.

- The investment level is **too low** at this stage in the product life cycle.

- The volumes are **too low**, and the fixed costs to collect and process are **too high**.

- This opportunity is not attractive because the size of the total addressable market is **too low**.

- Back in 1973, starvation was, in part, attributed to **low** harvests caused by a **too low** level of rainfall.

DESCRIBE

- One of the principal causes of project failure, for both regions, is often **a lack of** clarity on the exact scope and requirements.

- You operate with a collection of siloed systems and multiple platforms that cause inefficiencies and provide **too low** results.

- As a matter of fact, the performance of Buenos Aires is **too insubstantial**, but this is what we expected as a result of a continued price war.

- Your budget for research and development is **too low** compared with that of your competitors, and your **low level of innovation** reflects, among other factors, your positioning as a follower on the electronics market.

⇒ Too High

- Corporate taxes in **Canada** tend to be **too high**.

- In many ways, the discretion offered to unit managers goes **way too far**.

- Your customer acquisition cost is **too high** as compared to the competition.

- With taxes **too high**, we will retire from the run-up to new investment in the region.

- The distribution costs are **way too high**, and something must be done to cut costs aggressively.

- **Overestimation** of customer demand is one of the primary causes of project failure in this airline industry.

- This financing option isn't doable because the payments are going to be **way too high**, given the interest rates.

DESCRIBE

- Finally, our fixed overheads were ten percentage points above the budgeted figure, which is **too high overspending**.
- The **high** staff turnover, coupled with burnout and budget **overspending**, are the main causes of the project's poor performance after implementation.

⇒ Reaching Limits

- At this time, we are confronted with the fact that our business model **has reached its limit**.
- It's time to consider whether this growth model **was reaching its limits** in the food-processing industry.
- Unlimited, unregulated speculation on goods, commodities, and people **has now reached its limit** with the new regulation.
- Autonomous farm-level adaptation is **gradually reaching its limits** as climate change impacts become more and more drastic.
- The main takeaway of this discussion was that the existing company resources are **reaching their limits**, both financially and operationally.

⇒ Trapped In

- These economies end up **being trapped in** a cycle of poverty.
- The country **is trapped between** a possible future and a very outdated past.
- Companies **are feeling trapped** between the push and pull of innovation and costs.
- A dominant part of the population **is trapped in** poverty by inflexible welfare rules.
- Like many other poor countries, they have a poor education system - which **keeps** them **trapped in** poverty.

DESCRIBE

- Thousands of families living in rural villages and urban slums **are trapped in** a cycle of ill-health, poverty, and violence.
- If Tech Client chose not to pursue the 3D development program, **it might be trapped** forever **in** the brutally competitive tech market, unable to tap its real potential as an innovator.
- Emerging countries **are trapped between** the need to attract international investments to expand their telecommunications network, on the one hand, and social development goals on the other.

⇒ Not Feasible Given Constraints

- Growing the number of trucks to manage expansion plans **is not very feasible given** financial **constraints**.
- This attendance-based solution **is not** always **feasible, given** organizational and scheduling **constraints**.
- **Given** the time **constraints, it might not be feasible to** divide the time into two separate segments with two panelists.
- This approach **was not**, however, **practical or even feasible given** the time and resource constraints available for this engagement.
- We must be pragmatic about the outputs that are **feasible to** deliver **given** contextual **constraints** and past experiences in this industry.
- It would be a significant improvement for some donors but **might not be feasible due to constraints** in their public budgetary processes.

Exercises

1. Which two of the following expressions is not a result?
   a. achieved strategic goals
   b. meet objectives with tight resources
   c. will make good progress under uncertainties
   d. increased market share by 5%

2. Which of these expressions is not used to define a problem?
   a. best case scenario
   b. trouble is brewing
   c. a heavy cross to bear
   d. when the shit hits the fan

3. Give three expressions for:
   a. Facing Challenge
   b. Making change
   c. Monitoring

Chapter 6
ANALYZE

Use data to tell stories.

ANALYZE

Trends

⇒ Growth

Useful words to describe growth

to grow / a growth	to increase / an increase	to boost / a boost	to rise / a rise
to progress / a progress	to enhance / an enhancement	to expand / an expansion	to emerge / an emergence
to soar / a soar	to gain / a gain	to hike / a hike	to be higher than
to reach a peack	to go up	to boost	to improve

⇒ How does it grow?

- steady / steadily, substantially, sharply, fast / faster, rapidly, quickly, overnight, wildly, tremendously, markedly, steeply, roughly, straight, enormously, disproportionately.

- successfully, relatively, considerably, appreciably, extensively, noticeably, robust / robustly, consistent / consistently, solid / solidly.

- daily, weekly, monthly, quarterly, semi-annually, annually

- gradually, accordingly, slow / slowly, moderately, naturally, apace, commercially, continuously.

❞ Retail prices have **noticeably risen** during the last twelve months.

❞ Bernard Madoff's return stream **rose steadily** with only a few downticks in 17 years. (26)

❞ The perceived credit risk indicators **increased substantially** during the global financial crisis

❞ "In March 2007, the DJIA **sharply rose** by 157 points or 1.3%, after **dropping** more than 600 points from its **all-time high** of 12,786 on February 20." (27)

ANALYZE

⇒ Decline

Useful words to describe a decline

to drop/ a drop	to decrease/ a decrease	to decline/ a decline	to fall/ a fall
to shrink/ a shrink	to dwindle/ a dwindlement	to collapse/ a collapse	to diminish/ a diminition
to lower/ a lowering	to lessen/ a lessening	to mitigate/ a mitigation	to reduce/ a reduction
to weaken/ a weakening	to bottom out	to regress/ a regress	to decay/ a decay
to worsen/ a worsening	to be lower than	to plummet	to crash/ a crash

⇒ How does it decline?

- dramatically, substantially, steady/ steadily, sharply, fast/ faster, rapidly, quickly, overnight, wildly, markedly, steeply, roughly, straight, disproportionately, drastically
- relatively, considerably, noticeably, consistent/ consistently

ANALYZE

- daily, weekly, monthly, quarterly, semi-annually, annually
- gradually, accordingly, slow/ slowly, moderately, naturally, continuously

💬 The measure should limit the **worsening** of public deficits.

💬 The situation led to a **sharp decrease** in profitability and cash flows.

💬 The demand for this model has **dramatically decreased** ever since.

💬 The **rapid decline** in sales is actually due to a **dramatic drop in** prices.

💬 Our profits have only **moderately decreased** while others were losing millions.

💬 As funding **gradually dwindled**, every school within the target group suffered.

💬 Despite their great brand name, profits **dwindled significantly over** the past three years.

💬 It is too early to say when emerging market economies will **bottom out of the global financial crisis**.

💬 This **consistent drop** in our market share reflects the fact that more companies have set up in the region.

💬 Approximately 42% of households had seen their income **plummet** by more than 50% over the same period.

ANALYZE

⇒ Steady State

Useful words to describe a steady state

to remain stable	to be static/ statically	to level off	a stationary state
a stability	a steady state	a state of balance	to balance out
a balance state	a state of equilibrium	an equilibrium state	a stable state
a constancy	a dynamic balance	a stable condition	a stable model
a balanced condition	a balance	a continuity	a dynamic equilibrium

💬 Prices **have remained stable** during the last two years.

💬 Sales **have remained stationary** despite the marketing campaign.

💬 One has to make a reduction someplace or add more funds to **balance out** the budget.

ANALYZE

- At **stationary state**, the economy undergoes lower production levels, higher inflation, and an increased trade surplus.

- The oil market has **quickly returned to a state of equilibrium** after the OPEP members agreed to reduce production.

- The country's development towards a politically and economically **stable state** may be the key to resolving the conflict.

- Inventories had begun to **level off** earlier this month, but weak demand has prevented any significant reduction in the surplus.

⇒ Fluctuating

Useful words to describe a fluctuation

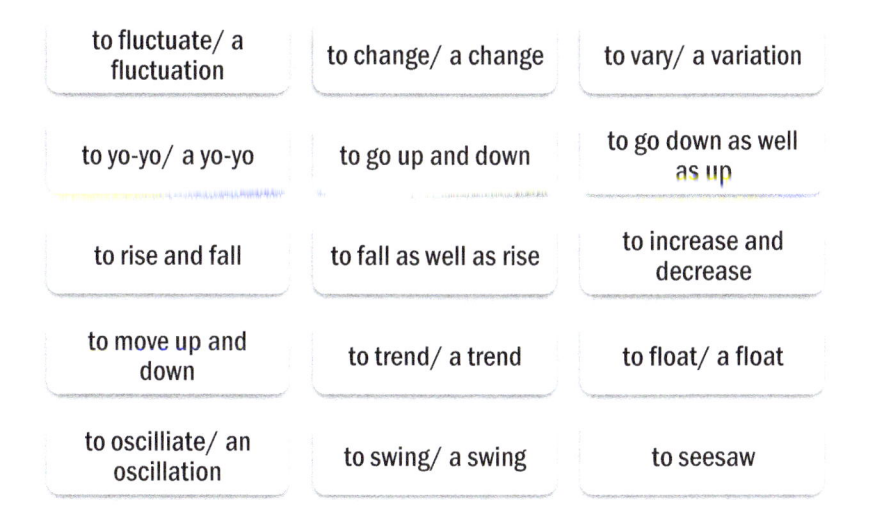

to fluctuate/ a fluctuation	to change/ a change	to vary/ a variation
to yo-yo/ a yo-yo	to go up and down	to go down as well as up
to rise and fall	to fall as well as rise	to increase and decrease
to move up and down	to trend/ a trend	to float/ a float
to oscilliate/ an oscillation	to swing/ a swing	to seesaw

⇒ How does it fluctuate?

- boom and bust, peaks and drops, peaks and valleys, upward and downward, on again off again, irregular, yo yoed, illness and wellness

- sharp, wildly, widely, dramatic, radically, sawtooth, rollercoaster, uneven, a lot, increasingly, decreasingly, upward, downward
- over time, from time to time, time-varying, in time, around, within, daily, weekly, monthly, quarterly, semiannually, constantly, independently, irregularly, seasonally
- with, in line with, according to, depending on, based on, upon, because of, with both, as, by

💬 The price curve has **floated over time irregularly**.

💬 The curve is **swinging** in a **boom and bust** pattern.

💬 The market **is going up and down** with no clear momentum.

💬 In the last three years, we have observed significant **variations** with **peaks and drops**.

💬 With intermittent periods of **illness and wellness**, what are the challenges of this industry?

💬 The high **fluctuation** of prices during the last five years has weakened the incomes of farmers.

💬 Stock prices are moving in a **rollercoaster fashion** since the announcement that the CEO is stepping down.

Analytical Engagements and Problem-Solving

⇒ Factors

- **The single most important factor** was the increase in the price of gasoline.
- The cost impact of the marketing campaign is **a factor** that needs to be borne in mind.
- The increased government spending will not be sufficient to **compensate for this factor.**
- The impact of a **change in one factor** may be compounded or offset by changes in **other factors.**
- **Single factors,** but especially the **combination of different factors** can better explain your reputation rundown.
- There must be enough adaptability to allow **this factor to be integrated into** the second phase of the project.
- The presence of **a single risk factor** may justify the conclusion that the country poses a high risk for factory operations.

ANALYZE

- In order to assess the causal effect of **single factors** on happiness, one needs to control for the **simultaneous effects of other factors**.
- The study found that household income is **one of the factors**, if not the **single factor**, that determine their chances of owning a home.

⇒ Objectives

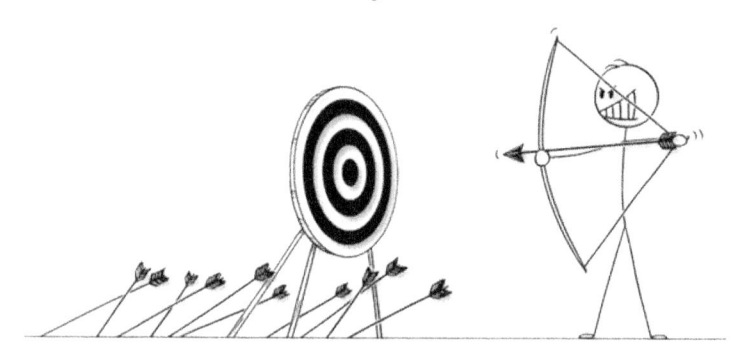

- The **aim should be** to have clients' feedback.
- The **primary objective is** to identify all the bottlenecks in sales.
- **Alignment between** operational and **strategic objectives** must be very clear to boost performance.
- The **overall objective** of this turnaround is balanced against the backdrop of continued innovation.
- The **overarching aim** of the framework agreement **is** to clarify the conditions for the final negotiations.
- Our firm will help you **meet clear business objectives** by breaking down and solving your biggest problems.
- The completion of the first functional prototype of the startup **remains the overarching objective** for 2020.

ANALYZE

- ◌ Alignment between business objectives and individual objectives is key to long-term career development for staff.
- ◌ The meeting will clarify the **overall objectives** of the survey and the direction the data gathering will take.
- ◌ **The primary objective** of the company is to continue creating value through optimal organic growth and the completion of successful acquisitions.
- ◌ **The primary objective** of this acquisition project meeting is to establish integration task groups composed of key persons from each of both organizations.
- ◌ **The overall goals** of the strategy are: (i) to reduce the prime cost to $2 per unit across all factories by the end of 2020, (ii) increase market share by 5% in two years.

⇒ Decision-Making Quadrant

High level of analysis

	Simple issue		Complex issue
	POOR over-analyzing, boiling the ocean	GOOD model, framework, brainstorming	
	GOOD intuitive, spontaneous, straightforward	POOR under- analyzing, unreliable	

Low level of analysis

ANALYZE

⇒ 4-Step Analytical Engagement

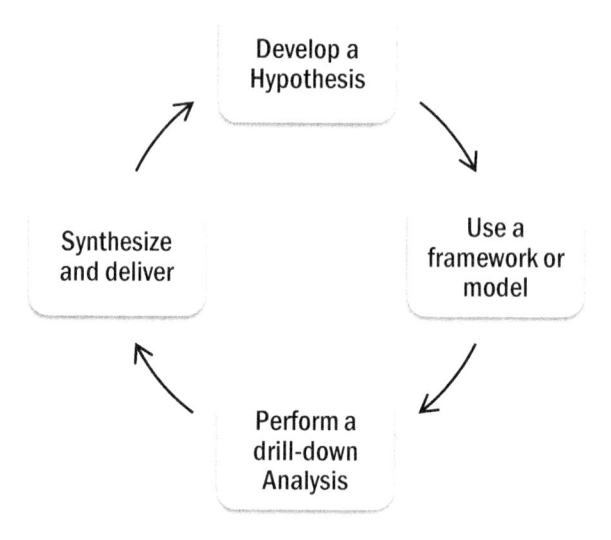

- Develop a Hypothesis
- Use a framework or model
- Perform a drill-down Analysis
- Synthesize and deliver

CASE 8: BIONADE's Market Entry in China (Fictive)

*****Important**: Kindly note that this sample case is *overly simplified and fictive*. The data might not be accurate or updated. It's given only for entertainment purpose. Actual engagements would need to be more elaborated and referenced as required.

Request for proposal

BIONADE is a German brand that manufactures nonalcoholic beverages. The Company offers fruit juices, diet drinks, refreshment drinks, soda, and other related products. The company was acquired in 2009 by Radeberger Gruppe. Its actual valuation is around €4 billion, and exports in more than 10 countries.

ANALYZE

BIONADE wants to enter the Asian market as part of a global growth strategy. The management of the company has set the priority on China. You will oversee the case and make both technical and financial proposals.

Develop a Hypothesis

The steady economic growth, coupled with a large customer base, makes the Chinese soft drink market an attractive one, and the German organic drinks producer BIONADE has the capabilities and competencies to serve this attractive market profitably.

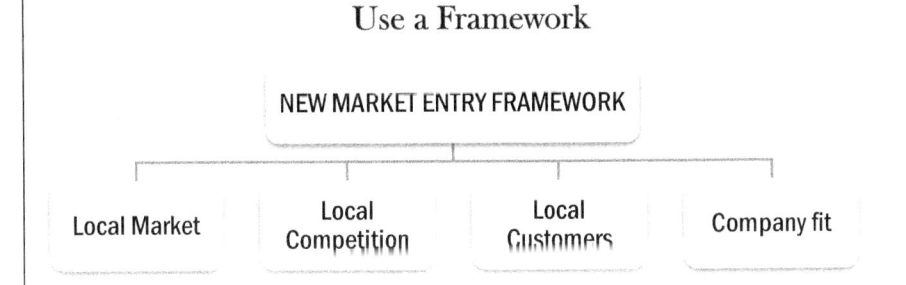

Use a Framework

```
            NEW MARKET ENTRY FRAMEWORK
    ┌──────────┬──────────┬──────────┬──────────┐
 Local Market   Local       Local      Company fit
              Competition  Customers
```

Basically, we should figure out whether the client should enter the Chinese market or not. If the conclusion is favorable, we will recommend the most appropriate entry strategy for the company's strategy and resources. There are 4 four areas we'll need to look at.

First, we will analyze the soft drink market in China to determine the trends and the annual growth rate. We will study the segmentation into non-carbonated and carbonated beverages as well.

Second, we need to have a good understanding of the competitive dynamics to find the count, positioning, and power of key players.

ANALYZE

The third bucket of this analysis relates to local customers. We need to grasp sub-drivers like tastes and needs, socio-demographics, income levels, and segmentation.

Finally, we are going to assess the client's fit with the Chinese market, assessing how its core resources and competencies will be a fit.

Perform the Drill-down Analysis

Market and Industry	Market size
	Growth rate
	Trends
	Segmentation
Local Competition	Key competitors
	Market shares
	Positioning
	Alternative competitors:
Local Customers	Customer types
	Segmentation
	Revenues and income
	Trends in customer needs
Company fit	Capabilities
	Core competencies
	Brand
	Customer loyalty programs

ANALYZE

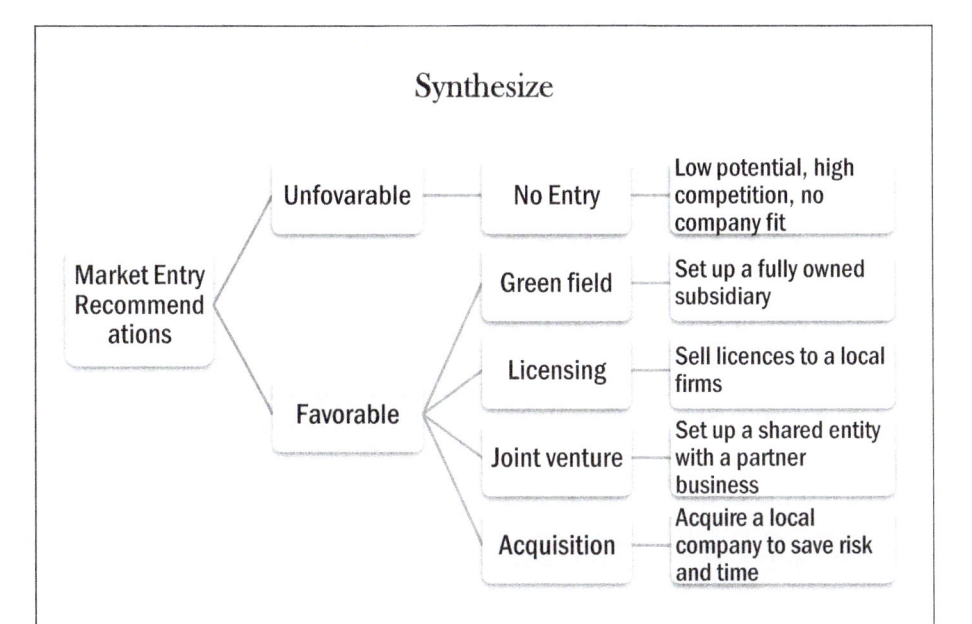

Synthesize

```
                          ┌─ No Entry ──── Low potential, high
              ┌ Unfavorable┘                competition, no
              │                             company fit
              │
              │            ┌─ Green field ── Set up a fully owned
Market Entry ─┤            │                 subsidiary
Recommend     │            │
ations        │            ├─ Licensing ──── Sell licences to a local
              │            │                 firms
              └ Favorable ─┤
                           ├─ Joint venture ─ Set up a shared entity
                           │                  with a partner
                           │                  business
                           │
                           └─ Acquisition ─── Acquire a local
                                              company to save risk
                                              and time
```

In conclusion, the client should proceed with the Chinese market entry by acquiring a local soft drink company for three reasons:

- The soft drink market in China generates $39b ($26b non-carbonated) in revenue annually, steadily growing at 8,7% per year, with 65% of sales driven by non-carbonated drinks (28). This rapid growth is four times higher than the growth rate in Germany. Healthy and natural beverages represent the major trends in customer preferences, which are the specialty of BIONADE.
- The market is dominated by Coca-Cola and PepsiCo, with respectively 42% and 32% market shares. German brands are associated with quality but suffer from a reputation of being expensive. Local brands like Wahaha or Tongyi are also well positioned with healthy soda, water, and fruit juice. BIONADE will be able to find its niche in healthy drinks.
- The Chinese market is different from the European and Canadian markets. The adoption curve is likely to be longer due to highly differentiated socio-demographics and business

ANALYZE

environment. Acquiring a local firm which is also making healthy drinks will save time and risk. The access to distribution channels and supplies will be easier for **BIONADE** if it acquires a well-established local firm.

All in all, that's why we recommend that **BIONADE** enter the market by acquiring a local firm. A detailed list of potential targets is proposed in the annexes section.

ANALYZE

Acronyms, Models, and Indicators

⇒ McKinsey Acronym Guide (29)

♞ AA

Advanced Analytics (in Excel).

♞ AP

Associate Principal. A middle position between "Engagement Manager" and "Principal." They cover 2 to 3 client studies while handling initiatives and proposals for future projects.

♞ APD

Advanced Professional Degree: JDs, MDs, and PhDs.

♞ ASC

Associate. Most are recent MBA or APD holders.

♞ BA

Business Analyst. Most are recent undergrads. They constitute the good deal of intellectual resources of every branch.

♞ CSS

Client Service Staff. Any "consultant" at McKinsey.

♞ CSSA

Client Service Staff Assistants – "Non-consultants" at McKinsey.

♞ CST

Client Service Team. It represents the engagement team members and all the leadership dealing with a client.

♞ CTL

ANALYZE

Counseled to Leave. As the Firm rarely lay off consultants, they can be counseled to leave, encouraged, and supported to find external opportunities.

♞ DGL

Development Group Leader. Partner in charge of a consultant's semi-annual review (SAR)

♞ EA

Executive Assistant. They perform support tasks, including expenses, agendas meetings, and trips organization. Only for McKinsey Directors, Sr. Principals, Principals, Associate Principals, and Engagement Managers.

♞ EM

Engagement Manager. It is the consultant in charge of leading the team on the ground. He or she supervises all progress of a client engagement day in and day out.

♞ IPM

In Production Mode. Meaning it's not finished yet.

♞ MECE

Mutually Exclusive and Completely Exhaustive. A fundamental principle creative problem-solving at McKinsey.

♞ PD

Practice Document. A PowerPoint deck available on McKinsey's "Know" repository giving the firm's most robust analysis on a particular subject.

Or any document from a directory of PowerPoint slides on a broad area of industry, function, and client subjects.

♞ PDM

Professional Development Manager. The manager in charge of enrolling consultants on client studies.

♞ PTO

Paid Time Off. The McKinsey term for vacation days or sick leave.

♞ SAR

Semi-Annual Review. It is the standard review process that is carried out every six months. The SAR rating of a consultant in the fall determines his or her annual compensation raise and bonus.

♞ SO

Significant other. It corresponds to a spouse, partner, boyfriend, or girlfriend of a McKinsey consultant.

♞ VGA

Visual Graphics America. A McKinsey subsidiary, located in the USA, and producing PowerPoint resources for McKinsey staff.

♞ VGI

Visual Graphics India. A McKinsey subsidiary, located in India, and producing PowerPoint resources for McKinsey staff.

⇒ Frequent Acronyms

- AAA: Alter, Avoid, or Accept
- AB: Annual Budget
- ABC: Always Be Closing
- ABM: Always Be Marketing
- ABP: Annual Budget Plan
- ACA: Apple Certified Associate
- ACAC: Agree, Confirm, Answer, and Close
- AER: Accurate – Efficient – Reliable
- AGR: Annual Growth Rate

ANALYZE

- AI: Artificial Intelligence
- AIDA: Attention – Interest – Desire – Action
- AIM: Answer-focused, Insightful, and MECE.
- AKA: Also Known As
- AOA: Analysis of Alternatives
- AOB: Any Other Business
- B2B: Business to Business
- B2C: Business to Customer
- BBD: Bigger Better Deal
- BBE: Barely Breaking Even
- BCS: Best Case Scenario
- BDA: Before, During, and After
- BEAT: Best Effort, Attitude, and Teamwork
- BI: Business Intelligence
- BOOT: Build, Own, Operate, Transfer
- BOST: Business, Operations, System, and Technology
- BP: Best Practice
- BRICS: Brazil, Russia, India, China, and South Africa
- BTOR: Back to Office Report
- BTW: Back to Work
- CAA: Competence, Agility, and Accountability
- CAC: Customer Acquisition Cost
- CAFE: Challenge – Adapt – File – Evaluate
- CAGR: Compound Annual Growth Rate
- CAPE: Capture – Analyze – Plan – Execute
- CAPEX: Capacity Expansion
- CAPM: Certified associate in project management
- CARE: Control, Analysis, and Risk Evaluation
- CBA: Cost-Benefit Analysis
- CBI: Critical Business Issue
- CBIS: Computer Based Information System
- CBOD: Corporate Board of Directors
- CCAR: Context – Challenge – Action – Result

ANALYZE

- CCIE: Cisco Certified Internetwork Expert
- CCNP: Cisco Certified Network Professional
- CCS: Care, Commitment, and Service
- CDP: Certified Data Professional
- CFA: Certified Financial Analyst
- CFE: Certified Fraud Examiner
- CFS: Critical Success Factors
- CGMA: Certified Global Management Accountant
- CHSC: Certified Health and Safety Consultant
- CIA: Certified Internal Auditor
- CIAO: Commitment, Independence, Attendance, and Ownership
- CIGC: Chartered Industrial Gas Consultant
- CIP: Continuous Improvement Process
- CIR: Consolidation – Integration – Redistribution
- CIS: Customer Information System
- CISA: Certified Information Systems Auditor
- CISM: Certified Information Security Manager
- CISSP: Certified Information System Security Professional
- CLTV: Customer Lifetime Value
- CMEMC: Construction Management Engineering and Materials Consultant
- CMFC: Chartered Mutual Fund Consultant
- CMFC: Chartered Mutual Fund Consultant
- CMS: Content Management System
- CMV: Current Market Value per share
- COGS: Cost of Goods Sold
- COS: Content Optimization System
- CPA: Certified Public Accountant
- CPA: Cost per Action
- CPC: Cost per Click
- CPF: Country Partnership Framework
- CPI: Consumer Price Index

ANALYZE

- CPL: Cost per Lead
- CPM: Cost Per Mile (YouTube)
- CR: Conversion Rate
- CRM: Customer Relationship Management
- CSR: Corporate Social Responsibility
- CTA: Call to Action
- CX: Customer Experience
- DAT: Decision Analysis Tool
- DEC: Design – Execute – Control
- DICE: Design, Innovate, Communicate, and Entertain
- DISC: Dominance, Influence, Steadiness, Conscientiousness
- DM: Direct Marketing
- DMAIC: Define – Measure – Analyze – Improve – Control (Six-Sigma)
- DMF: Design and Monitoring Framework
- DMS: Data Management Service
- DNDW: Do Not Deal With
- DNS: Domain Name Server
- DPO: Direct Public Offering
- DPR: Daily Progress Report
- DRIVE: Directional – Reasonable – Inspiring – Visible – Eventual
- DRP: Dealer Retail Price
- DRP: Disaster Recovery Plan
- DS: Direct Sales
- DSM: Daily Standup Meeting
- DTB: Don't Turn Back
- E&OE: Errors and Omissions Excepted
- EBIT: Earnings Before Interest and Taxes
- EBITDA: Earnings Before Interest, Taxes, Depreciation, and Amortization
- EDGE: Economic Dividends for Gender Equality
- EOD: End of the Day

ANALYZE

- EOW: End of the Week
- EPS: Earning Per Share
- EVA: Economic Value Added
- FDA: Food & Drug Administration (US)
- FOCUS: Frame, Organize, Collect, Understand, and Synthesize
- GAAP: Generally Accepted Accounting Principles
- HBW: Home-Based Work
- IAS: International Accounting Standard
- IFRS: International Financial Reporting Standard
- IPM: In Production Mode
- IPO: Initial Public Offering
- IPSAS: International Public Sector Accounting Standard
- IRR: Internal Rate of Return
- ISP: Internet Service Provider
- KB: Knowledge Base
- KPI: Key Performance Indicator
- LBS: Location-Based Service
- LTV: Lifetime Value
- M&A: Mergers and Acquisitions
- MCSD: Microsoft Certified Solutions Developer
- MCSE: Microsoft Certified Solutions Expert
- MECE: Mutually Exclusive and Collectively Exhaustive
- MoM: Month-over-Month
- MTA: Microsoft Technology Associate
- MTD: Month to date
- NDA: Non-Disclosure Agreement
- NPS: Net Promoter Score
- NPV: Net Present Value
- OCP: Oracle Certified Professional
- OOO: Out-of-Office
- OPM: Operating Profit Margin
- OPM: Other People's Money
- PER: Price Earning Ration

ANALYZE

- PERT: Program Evaluation Review Technique
- PESTEL: Political – Economical – Social – Technological – Environmental – Legal
- PIPE: Private Investment in Public Equity
- PIPE: Product Idea Profitability Evaluation
- PM: Project Manager
- PMP: Project Management Professional
- PPC: Pay per Click
- PPP: Public-Private Partnerships
- PR: Public Relations
- PST: McKinsey Problem Solving Test
- PTO: Paid Time off
- QoQ: Quarter-over-Quarter
- QR code: Quick Response barcode
- QTD: Quarter to Date
- R&D: Research and Development
- ROC: Return on Capital
- ROE: Return on Equity
- ROI: Return on Investment
- SaaS: Software as a Service
- SAM: Serviceable Addressable Market
- SEC: Securities and Exchange Commission
- SEO: Search Engine Optimization
- SG&A: Sales, General and Administration
- SLA: Service Level Agreement
- SMEs: Small and Medium-sized Enterprises
- SMM: Social Media Marketing
- SOM: Share of Market
- SWOT: Strengths – Weaknesses – Opportunities – Threats
- TAM: Total Addressable Market
- TEAM: Talk, Evaluate, Assist, and Motivate
- TORs: Terms of Reference
- UX: User Experience

- VC: Venture Capital
- WFH: Work from Home
- WOM: Word of Mouth
- YoY: Year-over-Year
- YTD: Year to Date

Exercises

1. Which is the expression that characterized a fluctuating state?
   a. a state of balance
   b. to balance out
   c. in a rollercoaster fashion

2. What is the meaning of the MECE acronym?
   a. Mutually Exhaustive and Collectively Exclusive
   b. Mutually Exclusive and Collectively Exact
   c. Mutually Exclusive and Completely Exhaustive
   d. Mutually Exclusive and Collectively Exhaustive

3. What are the elements of the 4-Step Analytical Engagement?

This page is intentionally left blank.

About the Author

My name is Adama Komou. I have worked for a couple of small and medium-sized consulting firms. I currently work at the World Bank. My field of competence cuts across start-ups, business development, project management, and finance.

I am currently completing a Master of Science in Finance and Investment at the London School of Business and Finance. I hold a bachelor's degree in Economics from the University Ouaga II.

I'd love to read your reviews for this endeavor to help me figure out how relevant it was. You can send your feedback directly to me at the email address below.

I will be delighted to make your acquaintance.

Yours truly,
Adama Komou
Email: adama_komou@yahoo.fr

This page is intentionally left blank.

Bibliography

1. **Haroun, Chris.** *Networking to Get Customers, a Job or Anything You Want.* s.l. : Haroun Education Ventures Inc., 2017.

2. **Thiel, Peter.** *Zero to One: Notes on Startups, or How to Build the Future.* New York : Crown Publishing Group, 2014. ISBN: 978-0-8041-3929-8.

3. **Jobs, Steve.** *Steve Jobs in 2010, at D8 Conference.* [Video] 2010.

4. **Schrage, Michael.** Knowledge Management. s.l. : Magazine, 2002.

5. **Governor, Andrew Cuomo.** Looking at possible APEX in 21 days. *CNN.* CNN, New York : CNN, March 27, 2020.

6. **Sinek, Simon.** *Start With Why: How Great Leaders Inspire Everyone To Take Action.* New York : Penguin Group, 2009. ISBN: 978-1-59184-280-41.

7. **Obama, Barack.** Leadership and World Change with Barack Obama. *GoalKeepers.* s.l. : GatesFoundation, September 2017.

8. **Canada, Library and Archives.** *Review of Governance Service Delivery: Audit Report May 2010.* 2010. ISBN 978-1-100-16001-6.

9. Consulting Glossary of Consulting Interview Training. *Street of Walls.* [Online] December 1, 2019. http://www.streetofwalls.com/finance-training-courses/consulting-interview-training/consulting-glossary/.

10. Glossary of Consulting Terms. *Glossary of Consulting Terms.* [Online] [Cited: December 4, 2019.] https://collaborate.uchicago.edu/depts/bcs/consulting/Consulting%20Resources/Glossary%20of%20Consulting%20Terms.pdf.

BIBLIOGRAPHY

11. Moore, Geoffrey A. *Crossing the Chasm: Marketing and Selling Disruptive Producst to Mainstream Customers.* New York : HarperCollins Publishers, 2014. ISBN: 978-0-06-229298-8.

12. 12 Startups that Failed this Year and Took $1.4 Billion in VC funding with Them. *Business Insider France.* [Online] November 4, 2018. [Cited: November 20, 2019.] https://www.businessinsider.fr/us/startups-failed-and-took-14-billion-in-venture-capital-funding-2018-10.

13. 32 of the BEST Value Propositions (Plus How to Write Your Own). *Optimonster.* [Online] [Cited: February 16, 2020.] https://optinmonster.com/32-value-propositions-that-are-impossible-to-resist/.

14. Home. *A-Z Acctax.* [Online] [Cited: February 16, 2020.] http://www.azacctax.com/.

15. Home. *Mint.* [Online] [Cited: February 16, 2020.] https://www.mint.com/.

16. 100+ Museum & Art Gallery Websites For Design Inspiration. *WhatPixel.* [Online] [Cited: February 16, 2020.] https://whatpixel.com/museum-art-gallery-websites/.

17. Salesforce: We bring companies and customers together on .... *Salesforce.* [Online] [Cited: February 16, 2020.] https://www.salesforce.com/.

18. Driving - uGO. *uGO.* [Online] [Cited: February 16, 2020.] https://www.ugointhecircle.com/transportation-options/driving.

19. Evernote | Smartsheet. *Evernote.* [Online] [Cited: February 16, 2020.] https://www.smartsheet.com/marketplace/apps/evernote.

20. Spotify works better with IFTTT. *Spotify.* [Online] [Cited: February 16, 2020.] https://ifttt.com/spotify.

21. Home. *Plated.* [Online] [Cited: February 16, 2020.] https://www.plated.com/?cvosrc=blog.morsel.typespeppers.

BIBLIOGRAPHY

22. InVision | Digital product design, workflow & collaboration. *InVision.* [Online] https://www.invisionapp.com/?ref=yesviz.com.

23. Jobs. *Glassdoor.* [Online] https://www.glassdoor.com/Jobs/Glassdoor-Jobs-E100431_P3.htm.

24. Christian. FOUR STYLES OF POLICY ADVOCACY PRACTICE. *AALEP.* [Online] July 29, 2015. [Cited: February 15, 2020.] http://www.aalep.eu/four-styles-policy-advocacy-practice.

25. Jansson, Bruce S. *Becoming an Effective Policy Advocate: From Policy Practice to Social Justice.* Belmont : Cengage Learning, 2014. ISBN-13: 978-1-285-06407-9.

26. HARRY MARKOPOLOS: WHISTLEBLOWER WHO EXPOSED THE MADOFF INVESTMENT SCANDAL. *People Pill.* [Online] [Cited: December 29, 2019.] https://peoplepill.com/people/harry-markopolos/.

27. Amadeo, Kimberly. 2007 Financial Crisis Explanation, Causes, and Timeline. *The Balance.* [Online] January 27, 2020. [Cited: February 20, 2020.] https://www.thebalance.com/2007-financial-crisis-overview-3306138.

28. Soft Drinks China. *STATISTICA.* [Online] August 2019. [Cited: March 29, 2020.] https://www.statista.com/outlook/20020000/117/soft-drinks/china.

29. McKinsey Acronym Guide. *Working With McKinsey.* [Online] http://workingwithmckinsey.blogspot.com/p/blog-page_16.html.

30. Johnson, Jana. Why is grammar important? *Daily Grammar.* [Online] November 28, 2019. http://ask.dailygrammar.com/Why-is-grammar-important.html.

31. Straus, Jane. Hyphens. *GrammarBook.com.* [Online] November 25, 2019. https://www.grammarbook.com/punctuation/hyphens.asp.

BIBLIOGRAPHY

32. Jamieson, Phil. Master Prefixes and Suffixes with Hyphens. *Proof Read Now.* [Online] December 8, 2017. https://www.proofreadnow.com/blog/master-prefixes-and-suffixes-with-hyphens.

33. Dodge, Kim. Beyond You're Welcome: More Ways to Respond to Thanks in American English. *English with Kim.* [Online] [Cited: 02 09, 2020.] https://englishwithkim.com/saying-youre-welcome/.

34. Annemarie. Better Ways to Say Thank You in English. *Speak Confident English.* [Online] May 2019. [Cited: 02 09, 2020.] https://www.speakconfidentenglish.com/say-thank-you-english/.

35. Alex. 17 ways to say YOU'RE WELCOME in English. *engVid.* [Online] [Cited: 02 09, 2020.] https://www.engvid.com/17-ways-to-say-youre-welcome-in-english/.

36. Management Consulting Glossary. *ConsultingFact.com.* [Online] 2018. [Cited: November 26, 2019.] http://www.consultingfact.com/blog/management-consulting-glossary/.

37. Vallabhaneni, Devi. *What Is Your MBA IQ? A Manager's Career Development Tool.* New Jersey : Wiley, 2009.

38. Sukhraj, Ramona. The 31 Best Value Proposition Examples You Wish You Had. *IMPACT.* [Online] August 14th, 2018. [Cited: February 14, 2020.] https://www.impactbnd.com/blog/value-proposition-examples.

39. Home. *Awesome Screenshot.* [Online] [Cited: February 16, 2020.] https://www.awesomescreenshot.com/.

40. CIPFA, Chartered Institue of Public Finance and Accountancy. *Management Accounting.* London : CIPFA, 2019.

41. How to Respond to HOW ARE YOU in English. *7ESL.* [Online] november 16, 2018. [Cited: february 22, 2020.] https://7esl.com/answer-how-are-you/.

BIBLIOGRAPHY

42. Angela Ackerman, Becca Puglisi. *The Negative Trait Thesaurus: A Writer's Guide To Character Flaws.* s.l. : JADD Publishing, 2013. ISBN: 978-0-9897725-2-5.

43. —. *The Positive Trait Thesaurus: A Writer's Guide to Character Attributes.* s.l. : JADD Publishing, 2013. ISBN: 978-0-9897725-1-8.

44. Les mots de liaison en anglais. *Wall Street English.* [Online] [Cited: 03 07, 2020.] https://wallstreetenglish.fr/fiches-anglais/vocabulaire/mots-liaison-en-anglais.

45. Andler, Nicolai. *Tools for Project Management, Workshops and Consulting.* s.l. : Publicis, 2011. ISBN 978-3-89578-671-6.

46. Holy Cow! 101 English Interjections and Exclamations. *Thought Co.* [Online] September 7, 2019. [Cited: November 22, 2019.] https://www.thoughtco.com/interjections-in-english-1692798.

47. Cheng, Victor. *Case Interview Secrets: A Former McKinsey Interviwer Reveals How to Get Multiple Job Offers in Consulting.* Seattle : Innovation Press, 2012. ISBN: 978-0-9841835-3-1.

48. Moore, Geoffrey A. *Crossing the Chasm: Marketing and Selling Disruptive Products to Mainstream Customers.* s.l. : HarperCollins Publishers, 2014. ISBN: 978-0-06-229298-8.

49. Kander, Diana. *All in Startup: Launching a New Idea When Everything Is on the Line.* Hoboken : Wiley, 2014. ISBN: 9781118857670.

50. 100 Events That Changed Business: 1900-2000. *TheStreet.* [Online] August 12, 2011. [Cited: 03 21, 2020.] https://www.thestreet.com/investing/stocks/100-events-that-changed-business-1900-2000-11173297.

51. 2010-2019 timeline contents. *FutureTimeline.net.* [Online] [Cited: March 21, 2020.] https://www.futuretimeline.net/21stcentury/2010-2019.htm.

BIBLIOGRAPHY

52. Bakhta, Sofya. Market research: The soft drink market in China | Daxue Consulting. *Daxue Consulting.* [Online] September 04, 2019. [Cited: January 18, 2020.] https://daxueconsulting.com/market-research-market-soft-drink-china/.

53. Overlong sentences. *University of Hull.* [Online] [Cited: October 12, 2019.] https://canvas.hull.ac.uk/courses/213/pages/overlong-sentences.

54. Zinsser, William. *On Writing Well, 6th edition.* s.l. : HarperCollins, 2001. 0-06-000664-1.

Printed in Great Britain
by Amazon